Patrick Proctor

The Encyclopedia of
Regional Chinese Cooking

The Encyclopedia of
Regional Chinese Cooking

**with recipes from Kenneth Lo's Chinese Cookery School
and Memories of China restaurant**

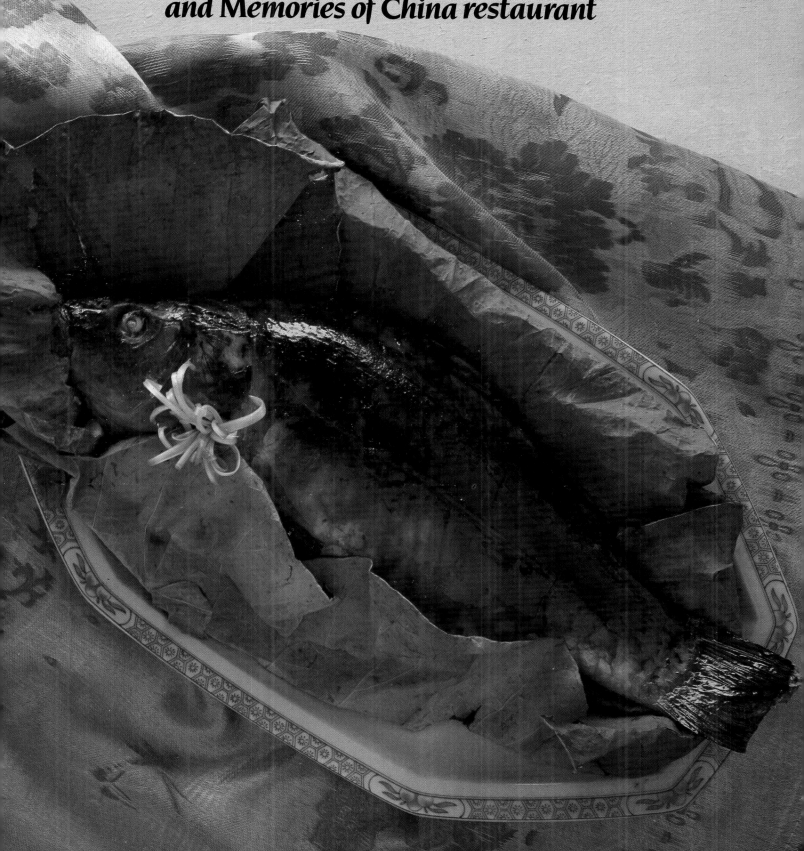

Contents

First published 1984 by Octopus Books Limited,
59 Grosvenor Street, London W1
This edition © Octopus Books Limited 1984

All recipes © Kenneth Lo and
Kenneth Lo's Kitchen 1984

All illustrations © Octopus Books Limited 1984

ISBN 0 7064 2179 5

Printed and bound by
Gráficromo, S.A., Cordoba, Spain.

Introduction

China, the third largest country in the world, stretches from the arid plains of Mongolia in the north to the sub-tropical climate of Yunnan and Kwantung in the south, where bananas and palm trees grow. To the west, its frontiers extend into central Asia, almost touching the border of Afghanistan, and from there its land mass stretches down towards the Pacific Ocean. On my last gastronomic tour of China we had to make six internal air flights and two railway journeys to cover all the territory and sample the different styles.

With such variation in climate and terrain, it is scarcely surprising that there should be an equal variation in the produce and cooking styles of the various provinces. This is a fact that the West is just beginning to appreciate, together with the paramount role that cuisine plays in the Chinese way of life.

Not everyone has the opportunity of visiting China, though the numbers are increasing every year – nearly half a million westerners last year. However, those who are left behind can take consolation in the fact that nearly all the foods one can eat or cook in China can be reproduced in a western kitchen. What Chinese cooking requires most of all is fresh food in prime condition, which is as easily obtained in the West as in China.

From the experience of my gastronomic tours of China I have come to the conclusion that nearly all the peculiar and highly exotic foods which are served in the more remote parts of China are of no great interest to the West. For instance, in the high altitude city of Kun-Ming in the deep south-west of China, we were served at one meal: Three Snakes Soup, Casserole of Braised Armadillo, Stewed Fruit-Eating Fox, Quick-Braised Ox Penis, and Braised Sea-Slugs with Crispy Meat Balls. Quite honestly, from a gastronomic point of view one could do without them!

As we travelled the length and breadth of China, we found that all the most appealing dishes were cooked from materials that are abundant in the West: the lamb and duck dishes of Peking, with the king prawns from the Gulf of Chili, the pears and chicken of Shantung, the chilli beef, venison, and crispy braised fish of Szechuan and the assorted fruit and vegetables, the fresh poached prawns, and the Cha Siu pork of Canton.

Unusual Ingredients

As for special Chinese ingredients (listed below) one hardly ever needs more than 10 or 12 of them. They are all easily obtained in the Chinese stores and supermarkets that can now be found in many provincial towns. In London, of course, there are three or four dozen of them. With their help you can launch into Chinese cooking with the fullest confidence and produce typical (and authentic) Chinese dishes.

Soya Bean Products

Soy Sauce Used extensively for flavouring or as a condiment or dip. Light soy sauce has a more delicate flavour and should be used for soups, fish and delicately flavoured dishes. When the colour is not specified in a recipe, this is the one to use. Dark soy sauce imparts a rich colour to food and is used for red-cooking for dark stews and meats.

Yellow bean paste or sauce Available in jars or cans in Chinese food stores. Often used instead of soy sauce when a thicker sauce is required.

Black bean paste or sauce Similar to yellow bean paste, only darker.

Sweet bean paste (also called red bean paste) Sold in jars or cans. Used as a dip, or to brush on to pancakes when serving Peking duck. Also used as a base for sweet sauces.

Salted black beans These are very salty indeed and need to be soaked for 5-10 minutes before use. They are then usually mashed into the cooking oil or sauce over high heat.

Hoisin sauce (also called barbecue sauce) A thick soy-based sauce with a sweet, hot flavour.

Bean curd Also known as *tofu*. An almost tasteless substance made from puréed yellow soya beans, which are very high in protein. It looks like junket, and is sold in cakes about 7.5 cm (3 inches) square.

Dried bean curd Also sold in cake form. It can be cut into strips or slices and stewed, braised or fried.

Bean curd cheese (fermented bean curd) Made by fermenting bean curd cubes in rice wine or salt. Available in two forms – white, or the Southern China red, which is more strongly flavoured. Both are very salty and strong-tasting.

Dried Vegetables and Fungi

Chinese dried mushrooms Widely used for their flavour and aroma. Soak them in warm water for 20 minutes before using.

Wood ears (also known as cloud ears) Dried grey-black fungi which should be soaked in warm water for 20 minutes before use. They have a crunchy texture and a mild flavour.

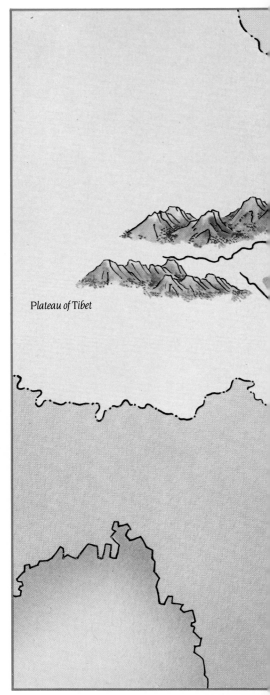

Plateau of Tibet

Straw mushrooms are completely different to other Chinese mushrooms in flavour and texture. They are only available canned.

Dried chestnuts Soak overnight in cold water then simmer in fresh water for 20 minutes.

Lotus nuts Available dried or canned in syrup. If dried, they should be soaked for 24 hours before use.

Lotus leaves Often used to wrap food before cooking, in the same way the West uses foil. The food is then usually steamed, the leaves imparting a special flavour to the food. The parcels are usually served whole and unwrapped at the table, the leaves being discarded afterwards.

Tiger lily buds (golden needles) They have a musky, slightly acrid flavour. Soak for 30 minutes in hot water before use.

Dried tangerine peel Gives a strong, orangey flavour to meats and stews. Soak for 20 minutes in warm water before use. You can dry your own.

Dried seaweed Sold in wads. When deep-fried in oil it becomes crisp and has a toasted fragrance.

Hair seaweed Fine black dried seaweed. A traditional ingredient of the vegetable dish Buddhist's Delight (page 164). It should be soaked for at least 20 minutes before use.

Canned Vegetables

Water chestnuts Available canned, ready peeled. They have a mild, sweet taste and a very crunchy texture.

Bamboo shoots (not to be confused with beansprouts) Available canned in large chunks. Often used in stir-frying to give texture to dishes.

Dried Fish and Seafood

Dried squid Tastes quite different from fresh squid and is regarded highly as a delicacy. Used to give extra

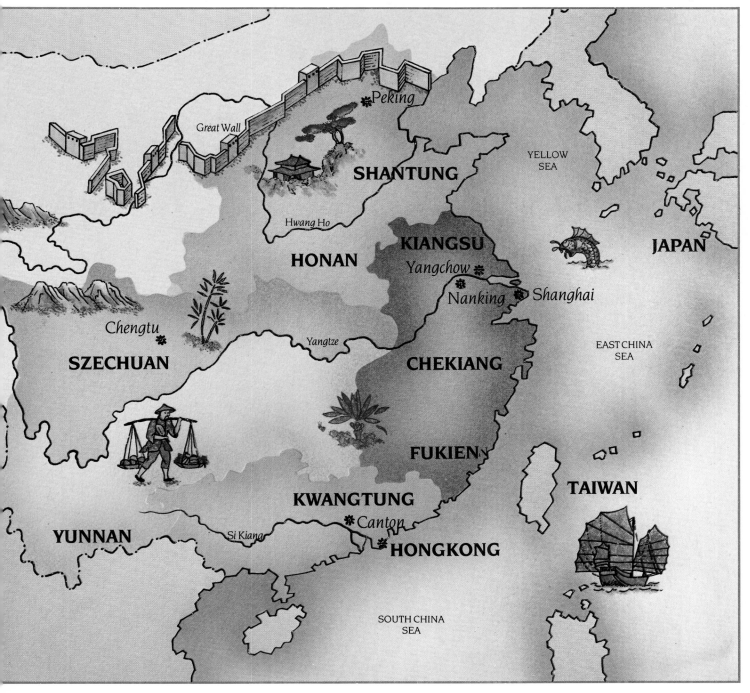

flavour to dishes. Soak before use in a solution of bicarbonate of soda, to soften it.

Dried shrimps Widely used to flavour savoury dishes. Soak in warm water for 30 minutes before use.

Fish maw Comes from the shark. Dried, it looks like a small yellow sponge, and has to be soaked for 2 hours before use.

Pickles

Snow pickle This is salted mustard greens. It is greenish in colour and has a mildly sour flavour.

Winter pickle Salted cabbage, brownish green in colour, is savoury and mildly salty. Sold in earthenware jars.

Szechuan pickle is hot and salty, with a peppery flavour. Often used to intensify the spiciness of a dish.

Sauces, Pastes and Oils

Chilli sauce A hot-tasting sauce made from red chillis. Similar in flavour to Tabasco. Greatly used in Szechuan.

Oyster sauce A thickish brown sauce made from soy sauce and oysters. Used mostly in the south.

Sesame paste Paste made from sesame seeds – very similar to peanut butter. Extremely rich and aromatic.

Sesame oil Widely used for its nutty, aromatic flavour. A few drops are often added to soups and other dishes just before serving.

Chilli paste A hot paste made of chilli, soya beans, salt, sugar and flour. Sold in jars. It will keep almost indefinitely.

Chilli oil The oil is made by frying small red chillies slowly in oil. The oil is reddish in colour and *very* hot.

Rice and Noodles

Egg noodles, made from wheat flour and eggs, can be round, like spaghetti, or flat ribbons. They can be bought fresh or dried in Chinese supermarkets. Italian pasta can be used as a substitute. Fresh noodles need a very short cooking time – 3-4 minutes.

Rice noodles (also called rice stick noodles) are white and thread-like. They can be found both round and flat, and are sold in packets in Chinese supermarkets.

Pea-starch noodles (also called cellophane noodles) or vermicelli, are white and translucent and resemble candyfloss. They should be soaked for 5 minutes before use.

Glutinous rice Round-grained rice used for stuffings and puddings such as Eight Treasure Rice (page 105). Pudding rice can be used instead.

Spices and Flavourings

5-spice powder A mixture of star anise, fennel seeds, cloves, cinnamon and Szechuan peppercorns. It is very pungent and should be used sparingly.

Ginger root Sold by weight. It should be peeled and finely sliced or chopped before use.

MSG (Monosodium Glutamate) also called Flavour Powder or Gourmet Powder. It is obtained from glutamic acid, which is present in a wide range of vegetables, and is also found naturally in the human body. It has little taste of its own, but possesses an amazing capacity to enhance the flavours of other foods. Its use in Chinese recipes is optional.

Szechuan peppercorns Reddish-brown peppercorns, native to Szechuan. Much stronger and more fragrant than normal peppercorns.

Star anise Dried, star-shaped seed head with a pungent, aromatic smell like fennel. One of the ingredients of 5-spice powder.

Basic Cooking Techniques

In China, there are 40 or 50 different methods of heat control (*he hou*) used in cooking. In practice, you need only be acquainted with a few of them.

Stir-frying Stir-frying is usually done in a wok. You can use a large thin-bottomed pan or frying pan instead, but the essence of the technique is that the food is cooked quickly, over high heat, in very little oil. The food to be cooked is finely sliced or shredded into similar sized pieces, using a very sharp knife or Chinese cleaver.

Shallow frying This is a slower method of cooking than stir-frying. Again, a wok or frying pan is used. More oil is used and the cooking is done over moderate heat.

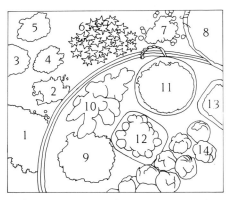

1. White peppercorns 2. Cloves 3. 5-Spice powder 4. Ginger 5. Nutmeg 6. Star anise 7. Lotus nuts 8. Tiger lily buds (golden needles) 9. Monosodium glutamate 10. Root ginger 11. Dried chillis 12. Dried chestnuts 13. Szechuan peppercorns 14. Garlic.

Deep-frying Deep-frying is used in the same way as in the west, to produce crisp-textured food. Sometimes the food is deep-fried, removed from the oil and drained. The oil is then reheated and the food deep-fried again, so that it is extremely crispy.

Paper-Wrapped Deep-Frying Small pieces of meat or fish are seasoned, then wrapped in cellophane paper to form little parcels, and deep-fried until tender. The food is served in its paper wrapping and opened by the diner with chopsticks. The paper is of course discarded. Cellophane paper is obtainable from large stationers.

Steaming The Chinese use bamboo steamers which stack on top of each other, so that four or five dishes can be steamed simultaneously. Dishes requiring most cooking are placed on the bottom layer, near the boiling water, while those requiring less are placed on the top 'floor'.

Roasting Used less in China than in the west as the average Chinese kitchen does not contain an oven : the best known dishes are restaurant ones, such as Peking Duck (page 47). *Cha Siu* is a method of quick-roasting meat or poultry at a high temperature for a short time.

Red Cooking This is a unique Chinese method, used primarily for cooking large cuts of meat or poultry. Dark soy sauce is used, which imparts a rich flavour and dark reddish-brown colour to the food.

Stewing Stews are usually composed of meat cooked on its own with herbs and spices, rather than with vegetables. In China, stews are usually cooked in an earthenware pot (called a sandpot) over a slow charcoal fire. The stew is cooked for a very long time – up to four hours – producing meat almost jelly-like in tenderness.

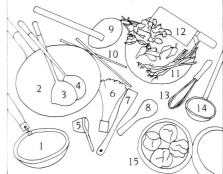

1. Rice scoop 2. Wok 3. Fish slice 4. Ladle
5. Bamboo strainer 6. Bamboo whisk 7. Scraper
8. Spoon 9. Wire strainer 10. Cooking chopsticks
11. Chopping board 12. Chinese cleaver 13. Whisk
14. Strainer 15. Steamer.

北部：北京

Patrick Procktor

The north of China offers a great contrast to the rest of the country: the environment is fairly bleak and the climate harsh for much of the year. The North China Plain, bordered by mountains to the north, stretches away in the west to the borders of Inner Mongolia. Spring and summer are dry and dusty, while the winters are freezing cold.

Wheat is the staple food, rather than rice. Wheat flour is used to make noodles, steamed buns, dumplings and pancakes. Meat is much more of a luxury up here and even vegetables must be stored over the winter. Dishes in general are much more plain, solid and nourishing.

Mutton and lamb are popular – no doubt due to the influence of the Mongolian invasion – though they are rarely eaten elsewhere in China. Mongolian Hot Pot (page 39) is a good example of the kind of cooking preferred – plain-cooked meat served with hot sauces. The strong flavours of leeks, onions and garlic feature largely. The most popular vegetable in this region is the Chinese cabbage, which can be stored over winter.

Peking, which lies to the north of the region, has been the capital of China for nearly 1000 years. The preparation and service of food became an important part of Court ritual and over the centuries the Imperial chefs brought about a great concentration of culinary expertise in Peking. This tradition is still evident in Peking cuisine today, which is lighter and more elegant than that of the outlying regions. Peking duck is of course the best known dish of all. In Peking ducks are specially bred for this dish and force-fed to just the right degree of plumpness and tenderness.

Shantung, the most southerly region of this province, is also the most productive. It produces the fruit and vegetables which also help to make this ideal chicken-rearing country.

The Yellow River, which flows across the North China Plain, is regarded as the cradle of Chinese civilization. (The earliest settlements were found along its banks). The river is famous for its carp, with golden yellow scales and delicate flesh. Of the many carp recipes to be found, Yellow River Carp (page 55) is one of the best.

In Chinese, *mu shu* means *yellow cassia blossoms. Mu Shu Rou is a very popular dish in Peking where it is often eaten wrapped in pancakes in the same way as Peking duck, accompanied by hoisin sauce. Menu serves 5-6.*

Mu Shu Rou

225 g (8 oz) minced pork
3 teaspoons soy sauce
2 teaspoons water
pinch of salt
pinch of freshly ground white pepper
pinch of MSG
5 tablespoons vegetable oil
6 dried Chinese mushrooms, soaked for 20 minutes, drained, stemmed and sliced
2 slices root ginger, peeled
2 tablespoons wood ears, soaked for 20 minutes, drained and sliced
3 spring onions, cut into strips
3 eggs, lightly beaten
2 teaspoons sesame oil
1 tablespoon dry sherry

Preparation time: 10 minutes, plus soaking and marinating
Cooking time: about 5 minutes

1. In a bowl, mix together the pork, soy sauce, water, salt, pepper and MSG. Leave to marinate for about 10 minutes.
2. Heat a wok and add half of the oil. Add the mushrooms and ginger and stir-fry together for about 1 minute. Add the wood ears and pork to the pan, stir-fry over high heat for about 2 minutes, then add the spring onions. Stir again, then turn out onto a serving dish and keep warm.
3. Add the remaining oil to the wok and reheat. Pour in the beaten eggs and stir over heat until the eggs have set. Return the pork, mushrooms and wood ears to the wok and mix with the eggs. Mix together the sesame oil and sherry and pour into the wok. Turn the mixture in the wok a few times to blend everything well, then serve on a warm serving dish.
4. Serve either with pancakes as in Peking duck (page 47) or with lettuce leaves.

Hot and Sour Soup

1.2 litres (2 pints) chicken stock
4 dried Chinese mushrooms, soaked for 20 minutes, drained, stemmed and shredded
5 cm (2 inch) piece bamboo shoot, shredded finely
2 cakes bean curd, cut into 1 cm (½ inch) cubes
50 g (2 oz) chicken meat, shredded finely
25 g (1 oz) frozen peas
½ teaspoon salt
pinch of MSG
2½ tablespoons wine vinegar
1 tablespoon soy sauce
pinch of freshly ground white pepper
3 tablespoons cornflour
6 tablespoons water
2 eggs, beaten

Preparation time: 10 minutes, plus soaking
Cooking time: 5-6 minutes

1. Heat the chicken stock in a pan with the mushrooms, bamboo shoot, bean curd, chicken meat, peas, salt and MSG. Bring to the boil and simmer together for 3-4 minutes.
2. Mix together the vinegar, soy sauce, pepper and cornflour and water in a bowl, and pour this into the simmering stock to thicken it.
3. Bring back to the boil, then pour the beaten egg in a thin stream onto the surface of the soup. Serve at once in a tureen or in individual bowls.

Steamed Chicken with Spring Onions

1 bunch spring onions, finely
   chopped
4 slices root ginger, peeled
2 tablespoons salt
2 tablespoons white wine
1 chicken, about 1.25-1.5 kg (2½-
   3 lb)
Sauce:
2 bunches spring onions, finely
   chopped
4 tablespoons finely chopped root
   ginger
6 tablespoons vegetable oil

**Preparation time: 10 minutes,
   plus soaking and marinating
Cooking time: about 1 hour**

1. Mix the finely chopped spring onions with the ginger, salt and wine. Leave to soak for 10 minutes.
2. Rub the chicken inside and out with the marinade and leave for 1 hour. Place the chicken on a heatproof plate, cover and steam for 50 minutes or until cooked. Turn off the heat and allow to rest in the steamer for an extra 10 minutes, then remove from the steamer and cut into small pieces. Arrange decoratively on a heatproof plate.
3. Mix together the finely chopped spring onions and ginger, and sprinkle over the chicken.

4. Heat the vegetable oil in a pan until smoking and pour over the chicken. Strain off the oil, reheat and pour over once more. Repeat for a third time, then discard the oil. Serve hot.

Left to right: Hot and Sour Soup, Steamed Chicken with Spring Onions, Mu Shu Rou

An *ideal dinner party menu as Drunken Chicken is prepared 2-3 days in advance. Menu serves 6.*

Drunken Chicken

醉

1.2 litres (2 pints) water
1½ tablespoons salt
2 medium onions, peeled and sliced
4 slices root ginger, peeled
1 chicken, about 1.25 kg (3 lb),
   trussed
600 ml (1 pint) Chinese wine or dry
   sherry

鶏

Preparation time: 5 minutes
Cooking time: 20 minutes, plus
   soaking

1. Bring the water, salt, onions and ginger to the boil in a large pan. Simmer for 5 minutes, then put in the chicken. Bring back to the boil and simmer, covered, for 15 minutes. Turn off the heat and leave the chicken to soak in the cooling liquid for at least 3 hours.
2. Remove the chicken and put into a stoneware jar or a casserole with a tight-fitting lid. Pour over the sherry or wine, completely immersing the chicken, and leave to soak for at least 48 hours. Turn the chicken every 12 hours.
3. To serve, drain off the sherry and untruss the chicken. Chop into bite-sized pieces, complete with bone, and serve as an hors d'oeuvre, eaten either in the fingers or on cocktail sticks.

Peking Sliced Lamb and Cucumber Soup

川羊肉湯

225 g (8 oz) boned lamb, cut into
   2.5 cm (1 inch) strips
1 tablespoon soy sauce
pinch of MSG
1 teaspoon sesame oil
1.5 litres (2½ pints) chicken stock
pinch of salt
pinch of freshly ground white pepper
1 cucumber, thinly sliced
1¼ tablespoons wine vinegar

Preparation time: 15 minutes,
   plus marinating
Cooking time: about 4 minutes

Left: Drunken Chicken

Right: Quick-Fried Shredded Pork in Capital Sauce, Peking Sliced Lamb and Cucumber Soup

1. Place the lamb strips in a bowl with the soy sauce, MSG and sesame oil and leave to marinate for 15 minutes.
2. Heat the chicken stock in a pan with the salt and white pepper. Bring to the boil, then add the lamb strips. Poach for 1 minute, then remove from the stock with a slotted spoon. Add the cucumber and bring to the boil once more. Reduce the heat and simmer gently for 2 minutes.
3. Return the lamb to the pan and add the vinegar. Bring back to the boil and serve at once.

Quick-Fried Shredded Pork in Capital Sauce

750 g (1½ lb) pork fillet, shredded
    into matchstick strips
pinch of salt
2 tablespoons soy sauce
1 tablespoon cornflour
1 tablespoon water
1 litre (1¾ pints) vegetable oil
3 tablespoons sweet red bean paste
½ tablespoon sugar
2 tablespoons sesame oil
2 tablespoons Chinese wine or dry
    sherry
1 lettuce, shredded

Preparation time: 20 minutes
Cooking time: 5-10 minutes

1. Mix the shredded pork with salt, 1 tablespoon soy sauce, cornflour and water and toss well together.
2. Heat the oil until it is smoking and add the pork. Stir-fry quickly for about 30 seconds, then remove and drain.
3. Mix together the sweet bean paste, sugar, remaining soy sauce, ½ tablespoon sesame oil and the wine. Heat 3 tablespoons of the oil in a pan until boiling, then add the combined ingredients. Bring to the boil and add the pork. Toss in the sauce and add the remaining sesame oil.
4. Place the shredded lettuce on a serving dish and place the pork mixture on top. Serve with noodles.

Serve the spare ribs as a starter. The 'Simulation of Crab' was invented by a chef for the Empress when crab was unavailable. The ginger and vinegar is served separately and stirred into the egg yolk and fish just before eating. Menu serves 6.

Spare Ribs with Black Bean Sauce

5 tablespoons vegetable oil
750 g (1½ lb) spare ribs, cut into
    5 cm (2 inch) lengths
3 tablespoons black bean paste
2 spring onions, finely chopped
2 thin slices root ginger, peeled and
    finely chopped
1 garlic clove, crushed
2 dried chillis, finely chopped
1 tablespoon Chinese wine or dry
    sherry
2 tablespoons soy sauce
1½ teaspoons sugar
2 teaspoons cornflour
1 tablespoon water

Preparation time: 15 minutes
Cooking time: about 1 hour
    10 minutes

1. Heat the oil in a wok until it is smoking and add the spare ribs. Stir-fry for about 2 minutes, then transfer the ribs to a heatproof bowl.
2. Pour off most of the oil, leaving about 1 tablespoon, and reheat. Put in the black bean paste, half the spring onions, the ginger, garlic and chillis. Stir-fry together for 30 seconds, then add the wine, soy sauce and sugar. Mix together, then stir into the bowl with the spare ribs. Place the bowl in a steamer and steam for 1 hour.
3. Pour off the liquid from the bowl into a pan and bring to the boil. Blend the cornflour with the water, and stir into the pan to make a smooth sauce.
4. Transfer the spare ribs to a warmed serving dish and sprinkle on the remaining spring onions. Pour over the hot sauce and serve immediately.

Empress's 'Simulation of Crab'

450 g (1 lb) white fish fillets, cut into
    matchstick-sized shreds
1½ tablespoons cornflour
8 egg whites, beaten lightly
250 ml (8 fl oz) vegetable oil, plus
    1 tablespoon warm oil
3 tablespoons chicken stock
1½ teaspoons salt
pinch of MSG
2 egg yolks
2 teaspoons finely chopped root
    ginger
2 teaspoons wine vinegar
sliced tomato, to garnish

Preparation time: 10 minutes
Cooking time: 8 minutes

1. Sprinkle the fish with cornflour and toss to coat evenly.
2. Add the fish to the egg whites and turn to coat each piece thickly, then add the warm oil.
3. Heat the remaining oil in a wok. Add the fish and fry gently until puffed. Lift out with a slotted spoon and drain on paper towels. Pour off the oil from the wok.
4. Mix together the chicken stock, salt and MSG. Pour this into the wok, add the fish and turn and stir gently over low heat for 2 minutes.
5. Place the fish on a well heated serving dish. Break the raw egg yolks over the fish. Mix the ginger and vinegar together and pour over the top of the yolks. Before serving, break the yolks and stir into the fish. Garnish with sliced tomato or radish roses, if liked.

Left to right: Peking Cha Chiang Mein Noodles, Empress's 'Simulation of Crab', Spare Ribs with Black Bean Sauce

Be sure not to overcook the fish: it should be white and translucent, to contrast with the egg yolks.

Peking Cha Chiang Mein Noodles

3 tablespoons vegetable oil
1 medium onion, finely chopped
2 slices root ginger, peeled and minced
1 garlic clove, crushed
225 g (8 oz) minced pork
½ teaspoon salt
½ tablespoon yellow bean paste
1 tablespoon soy sauce
3 tablespoons chicken stock
1½ tablespoons cornflour
1 tablespoon water
450 g (1 lb) egg noodles, boiled until
    just tender and drained

½ cucumber, cut into matchstick
    strips
3 spring onions, cut into 2.5 cm
    (1 inch) sections

Preparation time: 15 minutes
Cooking time: about 10 minutes

1. Heat the oil in a wok, then add the onion, ginger and garlic and stir-fry together for about 1 minute. Add the minced pork, together with the salt, yellow bean paste and soy sauce, and leave to simmer over low heat for 3-4 minutes.
2. Add the stock and cook for a further 3-4 minutes. Blend the cornflour with the water, then stir into the mixture and stir over heat until the sauce has thickened.
3. Put the noodles on a warm serving dish and pour on the meat sauce. Arrange the shredded cucumber and spring onions around the noodles and serve immediately.

Sesame Prawn Toasts are often served as a snack or hors d'oeuvre. The fish in wine sauce is a famous Peking speciality. The whiteness of the fish, immersed in a translucent sauce, contrasting with the jet black wood ears, makes this a very attractive dish. Serves 5-6 with rice or noodles.

Sesame Prawn Toasts

25 g (1 oz) pork fat, minced
125 g (5 oz) peeled prawns, minced
1 egg white, lightly beaten
pinch of salt
pinch of freshly ground white pepper
pinch of MSG
3 teaspoons cornflour
2 thin slices of white bread, crusts removed
75 g (3 oz) sesame seeds
600 ml (1 pint) vegetable oil

Preparation time: 15 minutes
Cooking time: 5 minutes

1. Mix together in a bowl the pork fat, prawns, egg white, salt, pepper, MSG and cornflour. Spread this mixture on to the bread slices.
2. Place the sesame seeds on a flat plate, then press on the bread slices, prawn side down, until thickly coated with the seeds.
3. Heat the oil in a wok to 180°C/350°F or until a cube of bread browns in 30 seconds. Carefully lower in the prawn toasts, spread side down, and deep-fry for 5 minutes, keeping them well immersed. Lift out and drain on paper towels, then cut each slice into 4 fingers. Serve hot.

Shredded Pork with Yellow Bean Paste

225 g (8 oz) pork fillet, shredded
2 egg whites
25 g (1 oz) cornflour
½ teaspoon salt
600 ml (1 pint) vegetable oil
1 tablespoon yellow bean paste
1 tablespoon Chinese wine or dry sherry
1 tablespoon sugar
1 teaspoon sesame oil
2 spring onions, cut into 2.5 cm (1 inch) lengths

Preparation time: 10 minutes
Cooking time: 3-4 minutes

1. Mix the shredded pork with the egg whites, cornflour and salt and toss all together.
2. Heat the oil in a wok until it is smoking, and add the pork. Stir-fry for about 2 minutes, then remove with a slotted spoon and drain.
3. Pour off most of the oil, leaving about 1 tablespoon to coat the bottom. Reheat the wok and add the yellow bean paste, wine and sugar. Stir all together and add the sesame oil. Return the pork and bring to the boil. Add the spring onions, toss together and serve immediately.

Top: Shredded Pork with Yellow Bean Paste
Bottom: Sesame Prawn Toasts
Illustration: Tea-picking in the 19th century.

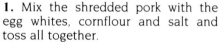

Peking Sliced Fish in Wine Sauce

糟溜魚片

450 g (1 lb) white fish fillets, cut into small thin slices
2 tablespoons cornflour
½ tablespoon salt
1 egg white
600 ml (1 pint) vegetable oil
2½ tablespoons lard
2 tablespoons dried wood ears, soaked for 20 minutes, and drained

Sauce:
4 tablespoons chicken stock
4 tablespoons Chinese wine or dry sherry
½ teaspoon salt
½ tablespoon sugar
1 tablespoon cornflower
1 tablespoon water

Preparation time: 5 minutes, plus soaking
Cooking time: 3-4 minutes

1. Rub the fish slices with a mixture of the cornflour and salt, then coat with the lightly beaten egg white.
2. Heat the oil in a wok then put in the sliced fish. Allow to cook very gently for about 1½ minutes (the fish should not be allowed to brown), then remove and drain on paper towels.
3. Melt the lard in a frying pan, add the wood ears and stir over medium heat for about 30 seconds. Pour on the chicken stock, white wine, salt, sugar and cornflour blended with the water, and mix all together. As soon as the sauce thickens, add the slices of fish, spreading them over the surface of the pan. Cook for about 2 minutes, then serve in a deep dish.

Right: Peking Sliced Fish in Wine Sauce

An *elegant dinner-party menu. Serve the Crystal Prawns as a starter, followed by the Chicken and rice. The Emerald Fried Rice could be served with any meat or fish dish. Menu serves 4-6.*

Crystal Prawns

225 g (8 oz) uncooked prawns, peeled and deveined
2 egg whites
1 tablespoon Chinese wine or dry sherry
pinch of sugar
1 teaspoon salt
pinch of freshly ground white pepper
50 g (2 oz) cornflour
600 ml (1 pint) vegetable oil
2.5 cm (1 inch) piece root ginger, peeled and finely chopped
2 spring onions, finely chopped
25 g (1 oz) frozen peas, lightly boiled and drained
1 tablespoon chicken stock
few drops of sesame oil

Preparation time: 10 minutes
Cooking time: 5 minutes

1. Put the prawns into a bowl with the egg whites, 1 teaspoon Chinese wine, the sugar, ½ teaspoon salt, the white pepper, and 40 g (1½ oz) of the cornflour. Mix together thoroughly.
2. Heat the oil in a wok. Add the prawns and stir-fry gently for about 2 minutes, then remove from the oil and drain on paper towels.
3. Pour off most of the oil, leaving enough to coat the bottom of the wok. Reheat the wok, then add the finely chopped ginger and spring onions. Stir-fry for a few seconds, then add the remaining salt, peas, wine, white pepper, chicken stock and remaining cornflour. Put the prawns back into the wok to reheat with the sauce. Pour into a heated serving dish and sprinkle the sesame oil over the top. Serve immediately.

Clockwise from the front: Emerald Fried Rice, Crystal Prawns, Shantung Hand-Shredded Chicken, Shantung Sauce

Shantung Hand-Shredded Chicken

5 slices root ginger, peeled and shredded
5 spring onions, chopped
3 tablespoons chopped coriander leaves
5 pieces star anise
1 tablespoon Szechuan or black peppercorns, crushed
1½ teaspoons salt
1½ tablespoons soy sauce
1½ tablespoons dry sherry
1 chicken, about 1.5 kg (3 lb)
1.2 litres (2 pints) vegetable oil
watercress to garnish

Preparation time: 15 minutes, plus marinating
Cooking time: 45 minutes

1. Mix together the ginger, spring onions, coriander, star anise, pepper, salt, soy sauce and sherry and rub into the chicken. Leave to marinate for at least 4 hours.
2. Heat the oil in a wok to 180°C/350°F or until a cube of bread browns in 30 seconds. Carefully lower the chicken into the oil and deep-fry for 5 minutes, or until golden brown. Remove from the oil and drain on paper towels. Then place in a steamer and steam for 40 minutes, or until cooked.
3. Allow the chicken to cool, then cut the flesh into strips. Arrange on a serving dish, garnish with watercress and serve with Shantung sauce (see below).

Emerald Fried Rice

225 g (8 oz) spring greens, finely shredded
2 teaspoons salt
5 tablespoons vegetable oil
3 eggs, lightly beaten
2 spring onions, finely chopped
450 g (1 lb) cooked rice
pinch of MSG
75 g (3 oz) ham, finely shredded

Preparation time: 15 minutes, plus soaking
Cooking time: 3-4 minutes

1. Sprinkle the finely shredded greens with 1 teaspoon salt and leave for 10 minutes, then squeeze out the liquid and chop finely.

2. Heat 1 tablespoon of oil in a frying-pan or crêpe pan. Pour in the beaten egg and allow to spread thinly over the bottom of the pan. When golden brown on the underside, turn over with a palette knife and cook the other side gently. Remove the omelette and cut into fine shreds.
3. Heat another tablespoon of oil in the frying-pan and add the finely chopped greens. Stir-fry for about 30 seconds, then remove from the pan.
4. Heat the remaining oil in a wok until it is smoking. Add the spring onions, then the rice, and toss well together until the rice is heated through. Add the remaining salt with the MSG, greens, omelette shreds and ham. Toss all together and serve hot on a serving dish.

Shantung Sauce

2 garlic cloves, finely chopped
2 chillis, finely chopped
2 spring onions, finely chopped
1 teaspoon sugar
1 teaspoon sesame oil
2½ tablespoons chicken stock
½ teaspoon salt
pinch of MSG
3 teaspoons dry sherry
2 teaspoons wine vinegar
½ tablespoon red chilli oil

Preparation time: 10 minutes
Cooking time: 1-2 minutes

1. Heat a wok, then add the garlic, chillis, spring onions, sugar and sesame oil. Stir-fry for 1 minute, then add the chicken stock, salt, MSG, sherry and vinegar. Stir over medium heat until boiling, then simmer for about 20 seconds.
2. Pour the sauce over the shredded chicken and finally drizzle on the red chilli oil.

The king prawns, with their tails left on for easy handling, are very decorative. Create a stir with the chicken, which gives an explosive sizzle as it is poured on to the red-hot iron plate. The Vegetables 'Wearing a Hat' is the original chop suey. Menu serves 4.

Peking Dish of Vegetables 'Wearing a Hat'

2 tablespoons vegetable oil
75 g (3 oz) shredded pork
3 tablespoons chicken stock
1 tablespoon Chinese wine or dry
    sherry
pinch of salt
pinch of sugar
pinch of MSG
3 dried Chinese mushrooms, soaked
    for 20 minutes, drained, stemmed
    and finely shredded
75 g (3 oz) peastarch noodles,
    soaked for 5 minutes, and drained
75 g (3 oz) bamboo shoots, finely
    shredded

50 g (2 oz) wood ears, soaked for
    20 minutes, and drained
100 g (4 oz) Chinese cabbage, finely
    shredded
75 g (3 oz) beansprouts
2 eggs, beaten

**Preparation time: 15 minutes,
    plus soaking
Cooking time: about 12 minutes**

---

1. Heat the oil in a wok, then add the shredded pork. Stir-fry until the pork changes colour and is almost cooked, then add the chicken stock, Chinese wine, salt, sugar, and MSG. Bring to the boil, then add the mushrooms, noodles, bamboo shoots, wood ears, Chinese cabbage and beansprouts. Stir-fry together for about 5 minutes, then drain off the sauce into the bowl. Lift the mixture into a separate bowl and keep warm.

2. Heat an oiled pan and pour in the beaten eggs to cover the pan thinly. Cook gently until golden brown underneath, then turn and cook for 1-2 minutes on the other side. Lift out and place on top of the vegetables, covering them completely. These vegetables can be served with pancakes, as in Peking duck (page 47).

Iron Plate Sizzled Chicken

鉄
版
鶏

1 teaspoon salt
pinch of freshly ground white pepper
pinch of MSG
1 egg white
225 g (8 oz) chicken breasts,
    skinned and cut into 2.5 cm
    (1 inch) slices
300 ml (½ pint) vegetable oil
3 stalks celery, cut into 4 cm
    (1½ inch) pieces on the slant
2 slices root ginger, peeled
5 tablespoons chicken stock
½ tablespoon cornflour
1 tablespoon water

Preparation time: 15 minutes
Cooking time: 10 minutes

1. In a bowl, mix the salt, pepper, MSG and egg white. Add the chicken slices and turn until coated.
2. Heat the oil in a wok to 180°C/ 350°F or until a cube of bread browns in 30 seconds, and add the chicken pieces. Stir-fry over heat for about 30 seconds, then remove from the wok with a slotted spoon and drain on paper towels.
3. Pour off the oil, leaving about 1 tablespoon in the bottom of the wok, and reheat. Add the celery and ginger and stir over heat for about 2 minutes. Add the stock and bring to the boil. Blend the cornflour with the water and stir into the wok to thicken the sauce. Return the chicken to the wok and stir for 20 seconds to heat through. Pour the mixture into a bowl or a deep plate.
4. Heat an iron skillet, griddle or tabletop burner until almost red hot. Bring to the table and pour on the chicken and celery mixture. It will sizzle and spit for a few minutes. Serve immediately.

Phoenix-Tail Prawns

鳳
尾
蝦

2 eggs
75 g (3 oz) plain flour
15 g (½ oz) self-raising flour
1½ teaspoons salt
1 slice root ginger, peeled and finely
    chopped
4 tablespoons water
600 ml (1 pint) vegetable oil
750 g (1¾ lb) uncooked king
    prawns, peeled and deveined but
    with tails still attached
To garnish:
parsley sprigs
lemon wedges

Preparation time: 30 minutes
Cooking time: 5 minutes

1. Beat the eggs, then add both lots of flour, salt, ginger and water. Mix together to form a light batter.
2. Heat the oil in a wok to 180°C/ 350°F or until a cube of bread browns in 30 seconds.
3. Holding them by the tail, dip the prawns into the batter, then lower them into the oil. Deep-fry for about 3 minutes or until golden brown. Remove from the oil and drain on paper towels.
4. Reheat the oil and fry the prawns again for 30 seconds to crisp. Serve hot, garnished with parsley and lemon wedges.

Left to right: Peking Dish of Vegetables 'Wearing a Hat', Phoenix-Tail Prawns, Iron Plate Sizzled Chicken

If liked, the prawns can be served with a dip: Mix together 1½ tablespoons hot chilli sauce, 2 tablespoons soy sauce, 1 tablespoon wine vinegar, 2 garlic cloves, crushed, and 1 tablespoon of finely chopped spring onion.

This menu will serve 4-6, with the addition of fried rice or noodles.

White Braised Cabbage

2 tablespoons vegetable oil
1 large Chinese cabbage, cut roughly
  into 8 pieces
1 teaspoon salt
2 slices root ginger, peeled
25 g (1 oz) dried shrimps, soaked for
  20 minutes and drained
250 ml (8 fl oz) chicken stock
pinch of MSG
1 tablespoon cornflour
2 tablespoons white wine

**Preparation time: 5 minutes,
  plus soaking
Cooking time: 20 minutes**

1. Heat the oil in a pan and add the cabbage pieces. Sprinkle with salt. Turn the cabbage to coat it with the oil and add the ginger, dried shrimps and half the chicken stock. Cover and simmer gently for 15 minutes.
2. Mix together the MSG, cornflour and remaining stock and pour over the cabbage pieces. Add the wine and turn the cabbage carefully so it is coated in sauce but not broken up. Simmer for 5 minutes.
3. Carefully lift out the cabbage pieces and arrange on a serving dish as near as possible to the original shape. Pour over the sauce and serve.

Garlic Chicken

225 g (8 oz) chicken breasts,
  skinned and thinly sliced
2 egg whites
pinch of freshly ground white pepper
pinch of salt
4½ tablespoons cornflour
½ teaspoon sugar, plus a pinch
600 ml (1 pint) vegetable oil
4 garlic cloves, crushed
4½ tablespoons chicken stock
1 tablespoon Chinese wine or dry
  sherry
pinch of MSG
½ cucumber, peeled, seeded and
  thinly sliced
few drops of chilli oil

**Preparation time: 15 minutes
Cooking time: about 10 minutes**

1. Place the chicken slices in a bowl with the egg whites, white pepper, salt, 4 tablespoons cornflour and pinch of sugar and toss well.
2. Heat the oil in a wok, add the chicken and fry gently for a few minutes, then drain on paper towels.
3. Pour off the oil, leaving 1 tablespoon. Reheat the wok, add the garlic and fry briefly. Add 4 tablespoons stock, wine, remaining sugar and MSG. Bring to the boil, then add the chicken and cucumber. Blend the remaining cornflour and stock and stir into the sauce until it thickens. Sprinkle with chilli oil.

Triple Quick Fry

3 tablespoons vegetable oil
225 g (8 oz) veal or pork kidneys,
  skinned, cored and cut into
  1 cm (½ inch) cubes
225 g (8 oz) veal or pork, cut into 1
  cm (½ inch) cubes
100 g (4 oz) veal or pork liver, cut
  into 1 cm (½ inch) cubes
1½ tablespoons yellow bean sauce
1½ tablespoons soy sauce
2 tablespoons hoisin sauce
1 tablespoon cornflour
1 tablespoon water
1 tablespoon finely chopped spring
  onion

**Preparation time: 10 minutes
Cooking time: 5 minutes**

1. Heat the oil in a wok until smoking, then add the meat cubes and stir-fry quickly over high heat for about 2 minutes. Remove and drain on paper towels.
2. Reheat the wok, add the yellow bean sauce, soy sauce and hoisin sauce and bring to the boil. Blend the cornflour with the water and stir into the wok to thicken the sauce.
3. Return the meat to the wok. Toss to coat in the sauce and reheat. Serve immediately, sprinkled with the spring onion.

*Clockwise from the front: Garlic Chicken,
White Braised Cabbage, Triple Quick Fry*

Crispy rice is made from leftover cooked rice, preferably rice that has stuck to the bottom of the pan. Allow to dry overnight, or dry it off in a low oven before placing in the hot oil. This menu serves 4.

Prawns on Crispy Rice

蝦
仁
鍋
巴

175 g (6 oz) uncooked prawns,
    peeled and deveined
50 g (2 oz) cornflour
1 egg white
600 ml (1 pint) vegetable oil
175 g (6 oz) crispy rice
900 ml (1½ pints) chicken stock
50 g (2 oz) frozen green beans,
    thawed and diced
75 g (3 oz) canned straw
    mushrooms, sliced
5 cm (2 inch) piece canned bamboo
    shoot, thinly sliced
15 g (½ oz) sugar
pinch of MSG
2 spring onions, finely chopped
3 tablespoons tomato ketchup

Preparation time: 10 minutes
Cooking time: about 10 minutes

1. Toss the prawns in a bowl with the cornflour and egg white.
2. Heat the oil in a wok to 180°C/350°F or until a cube of bread browns in 30 seconds, and carefully put in the crispy rice. This should sizzle and puff up immediately. Remove from the oil and drain on paper towels. Put the rice into a bowl.
3. Reheat the oil and then put in the prawns. Stir-fry gently for about 2 minutes, then remove and drain on paper towels. Keep warm.
4. Pour off most of the oil, leaving about 1 tablespoon in the bottom. Reheat the wok and pour in the chicken stock. Bring to the boil, then add the green beans, straw mushrooms, bamboo shoots, salt, sugar, MSG, spring onions and tomato ketchup and simmer for 4-5 minutes.
5. When ready to serve, place the prawns on top of the crispy rice and pour on the soup. Serve immediately.

Shredded Lamb with Spring Onions

慈
爆
羊
肉

450 g (1 lb) boneless lamb, shredded
1 tablespoon Chinese wine or dry
    sherry
1 teaspoon salt
1 egg white
50 g (2 oz) cornflour, plus
    1 teaspoon
300 ml (½ pint) vegetable oil
225 g (8 oz) spring onions, cut into
    2.5 cm (1 inch) pieces
2 garlic cloves, crushed
1 teaspoon sugar
½ teaspoon freshly ground white
    pepper
2 teaspoons soy sauce
2 tablespoons water
1 teaspoon sesame oil
1 tablespoon dry English mustard

Preparation time: 15 minutes
Cooking time: 4-5 minutes

1. Mix the shredded lamb with the wine, half the salt, the egg white and 50 g (2 oz) cornflour and toss well.
2. Heat the oil in a wok until smoking, and add the shredded lamb. Stir-fry for about 2 minutes, then remove with a slotted spoon and drain on paper towels.
3. Pour off most of the oil, leaving only about 1 tablespoon to coat the wok. Reheat, then put in the spring onions, garlic, remaining salt, sugar, white pepper and soy sauce. Bring to the boil. Blend together 1 teaspoon cornflour with 2 tablespoons water and add to the wok to thicken the sauce, then put the lamb back in to reheat.
4. Spoon the lamb mixture on to a serving dish, and sprinkle with the sesame oil. Serve with the mustard and remaining water blended to form a dip sauce.

Red-Cooked Cabbage

紅
燒
白
菜

1.25 kg (2½ lb) Chinese cabbage,
   cut crosswise into 4 cm (1½ inch)
   pieces
3 tablespoons dark soy sauce
2 teaspoons sugar
½ teaspoon salt
3 tablespoons dry sherry
1 teaspoon MSG
4 tablespoons beef stock
1 dried chilli, seeded and sliced
2 spring onions, cut into 2½ cm
   (1 inch) pieces
4 tablespoons vegetable oil
3 dried Chinese mushrooms, soaked
   for 20 minutes, drained, stemmed
   and shredded

Preparation time: 15 minutes,
   plus soaking
Cooking time: about 20 minutes

1. Wash and dry the cabbage pieces.
In a bowl, mix together the soy sauce,
sugar, salt and sherry. In another
bowl, blend the MSG with the stock.
2. Heat the oil in a wok then add the
chilli and spring onions. Stir-fry for
1-2 minutes then remove the chilli
and discard. Add the cabbage and
mushrooms and stir-fry over medium
heat for 5 minutes.
3. Pour the soy sauce mixture into
the wok. Stir-fry for a further minute,
then reduce the heat and simmer
gently for 10 minutes, turning the
cabbage pieces a few times. Add the
stock and stir and turn a few more
times, until the sauce thickens.

*Left to right: Shredded Lamb with Spring
Onions, Red-Cooked Cabbage, Prawns on
Crispy Rice*

Illustration: Blindfolded mules
husking rice.

A typical hearty, filling meal from the north. The lard gives the pancakes an authentic savoury flavour. Serve with a fresh-tasting salad, such as beansprouts. Menu serves 4.

Shredded Pork with Sweet Bean Paste Over Puffy Rice Noodles

醬
爆
肉
絲
炸
粉

450 g (1 lb) lean pork, shredded
1 tablespoon soy sauce
1 tablespoon Chinese wine or dry
   sherry
½ teaspoon salt
½ teaspoon freshly ground white
   pepper
½ teaspoon ground ginger
2½ tablespoons sweet bean paste
600 ml (1 pint) vegetable oil
50 g (2 oz) rice noodles
1 large leek, shredded

Preparation time: 15 minutes
Cooking time: 3-4 minutes

1. Mix the shredded pork in a bowl with the soy sauce, wine, salt, pepper, ginger and sweet bean paste.
2. Heat the oil in a wok to 180°C/350°F, or until a cube of bread browns in 30 seconds, and add the rice noodles. They should puff up immediately. Remove from the heat and drain on paper towels.
3. Pour off most of the oil, leaving about 1 tablespoon in the bottom of the wok. Reheat the wok and add the shredded leek. Stir-fry quickly for about 1 minute, then transfer to a serving dish and surround with the crispy noodles.
4. Put another 4 tablespoons of oil into the wok and reheat. Add the meat, and stir-fry for 4-5 minutes or until the colour changes. Spoon the meat on top of the leeks and serve immediately.

Onion Pancakes

450 g (1 lb) plain flour
250 ml (8 fl oz) boiling water
300 ml (½ pint) cold boiled water
450 g (1 lb) onions, peeled and
    finely chopped
5 tablespoons lard or vegetable oil
1½ tablespoons salt

**Preparation time: 20 minutes,
   plus resting
Cooking time: 4 minutes**

1. Sift the flour into a bowl. Pour in the boiling water, stirring all the time to form a stiff dough. Add the cold water to the dough and when it is cool enough to handle, knead until smooth. Cover the dough and leave to rest for about 30 minutes.
2. Roll the dough into a long sausage and cut into 10 pieces. Roll each piece into a ball, then flatten with the rolling pin into a small pancake about 7.5-10 cm (3-4 inches) in diameter. Sprinkle each pancake with the chopped onion and salt. Fold the edges of the pancake into the middle and then roll out into a pancake again.
3. Heat 2 tablespoons of lard in a frying pan and put in the pancakes. Fry in batches for 2 minutes on either side, or until golden brown, adding more lard as necessary.
4. Serve hot either by themselves or as an accompaniment to savoury foods.

Left: *Shredded Pork with Sweet Bean Paste over Puffy Rice Noodles*
Right: *Onion Pancakes*
Illustration: Street trader with a portable stove.

An elegant menu for a special occasion. The king prawns served with a tomato dip sauce make an impressive starter. Serve plain or fried rice, or Northern Fried Noodles (page 44), to complement the elegant main dishes: Deep-Fried Chicken, served with colourful peppers and water chestnuts in a delicately flavoured, yellow-tinted sauce, and Peking Meat Balls, served on a bed of lettuce leaves and garnished with orange or lemon slices. Steamed Pears in Syrup (page 58) with its pretty pink coloured sauce would be the ideal dessert to round off this meal. Menu serves 4.

Hot-Fried King Prawns in Breadcrumbs

8 uncooked king prawns, peeled and
   deveined and cut in half down the
   back
50 g (2 oz) seasoned flour, for
   dusting
3 egg whites
pinch of cornflour
4 tablespoons breadcrumbs
600 ml (1 pint) vegetable oil
6 tablespoons tomato purée

Preparation time: 10 minutes
Cooking time: 3-4 minutes

1. Dust the king prawns with the seasoned flour.
2. Beat the egg whites lightly, then beat in the cornflour. Coat the prawns thickly with this mixture, then dip in breadcrumbs.

3. Heat the vegetable oil in a wok to 180°C/350°F or until a cube of bread browns in 30 seconds. Put in the coated prawns and deep-fry for about 3 minutes or until golden brown, then remove from the oil and drain on paper towels.
4. Place the prawns on a warm serving dish and use the tomato purée as a dip.

Deep-Fried Chicken with Lemon Sauce

1 teaspoon salt
1 tablespoon Chinese wine or dry sherry
½ tablespoon light soy sauce
2 tablespoons cornflour
1 tablespoon water
1 egg yolk
pinch of freshly ground white pepper
450 g (1 lb) chicken meat, skinned and cut into 2.5 cm (1 inch) slices
600 ml (1 pint) vegetable oil, plus 2 tablespoons
1 green pepper, cored, seeded and cut into 2.5 cm (1 inch) pieces
1 red pepper, cored, seeded and cut into 2.5 cm (1 inch) pieces
100 g (4 oz) canned water chestnuts, drained and thinly sliced
3 tablespoons sugar
4 tablespoons lemon juice
6 tablespoons chicken stock
1 tablespoon sesame oil
3 drops yellow food colouring
1 lemon, sliced, to garnish
fresh coriander leaves, to garnish

Preparation time: 10 minutes, plus marinating
Cooking time: about 5 minutes

1. Mix together half the salt, the wine, soy sauce, 1 tablespoon cornflour, the water, egg yolk and a pinch of pepper, add the chicken slices and marinate for 10 minutes.
2. Heat the oil in a wok to 180°C/350°F, or until a cube of bread browns in 30 seconds, and deep-fry the chicken slices until golden brown. Remove and drain on paper towels.
3. Heat 1 tablespoon oil in another wok. Add the peppers and water chestnuts. Stir-fry until they change colour, then transfer to a heated serving dish.
4. Wipe the wok clean with paper towels and add another tablespoon of oil. Reheat and stir in the sugar, lemon juice, chicken stock, remaining salt, remaining cornflour, sesame oil and yellow food colouring. Bring to the boil, stirring all the time.
5. Reheat the oil and fry the chicken again for 10 seconds to reheat. Drain and place on top of the peppers and water chestnuts. Pour the sauce on top and garnish with lemon slices and coriander leaves.

Peking Meat Balls

450 g (1 lb) minced pork
25 g (1 oz) dried Chinese mushrooms, soaked for 20 minutes, drained, stemmed and finely chopped
50 g (2 oz) peeled prawns, minced
2 spring onions, finely chopped
2.5 cm (1 inch) piece root ginger, peeled and finely chopped
2 eggs
1 tablespoon Chinese wine or dry sherry
pinch of MSG
½ teaspoon sesame oil
1 teaspoon salt
3 tablespoons cornflour
600 ml (1 pint) vegetable oil
To serve:
lettuce leaves
1 orange or lemon, thinly sliced

Preparation time: 20 minutes, plus soaking
Cooking time: about 5 minutes

1. In a bowl, mix together the pork, Chinese mushrooms, prawns, spring onions, ginger and eggs. Add to this the Chinese wine, MSG, sesame oil, salt and cornflour. Mix everything together thoroughly, then roll into small balls using about 2 teaspoons per ball.
2. Heat the oil in a wok to 180°C/350°F, or until a cube of bread browns in 30 seconds, then put in the meatballs. Fry until golden brown all over, then remove with a slotted spoon and drain on paper towels. Serve on lettuce leaves, surrounded by a thinly sliced lemon or orange.

Left: Hot-Fried King Prawns in Breadcrumbs
Top: Deep-Fried Chicken with Lemon Sauce
Bottom: Peking Meat Balls

The classic Peking dish. The fire-pot has a central funnel which is filled with burning charcoal. The 'moat' is filled with hot stock in which the cooking is done (rather like a fondue). Fire-pots can be bought in Chinese supermarkets. Serves 8-12.

Mongolian Hot-Pot

2 litres (3½ pints) *beef stock*
2 slices *root ginger, finely chopped*
3 *spring onions, finely chopped*
450 g (1 lb) *Chinese cabbage, shredded*
450 g (1 lb) *spinach, shredded*
225 g (8 oz) *mushrooms, sliced*
2 cakes *bean curd, sliced*
225 g (8 oz) *cellophane noodles, soaked and drained*
2 kg (4 lb) *lamb or beef fillet, cut into paper-thin slices*
Dips:
4 tablespoons *dark soy sauce*
1 tablespoon *chilli sauce*
3 tablespoons *hoisin sauce*
2 tablespoons *salt*
3 tablespoons *wine vinegar, mixed with 3 tablespoons finely chopped coriander*

Preparation time: 35-40 minutes

1. Bring the stock to a boil, add the ginger and spring onions, and 3 tablespoons each of the vegetables, bean curd and the noodles.
2. Arrange the dips in individual little dishes. Each person makes up his own dip from the various sauces.
3. Each person picks up a piece of meat and dips it into the boiling liquid – as soon as the colour of the meat changes it is done. He then retrieves it, together with some vegetables and noodles, dips them in the sauce and eats it while piping hot.
4. More vegetables are added as required. When all the meat has been eaten, the remainder of the vegetables, bean curd and noodles are added to the soup. Boil vigorously for 3-4 minutes, then ladle into individual bowls and serve as soup.

Mongolian Hot-Pot with dip sauces

In the north these dumplings often constitute a meal on their own, served with vinegar or soy sauce dips, together with a soup made from the water in which the dumplings were boiled. Here, the addition of Mongolian Lamb Puffs makes a more exciting meal. Rice or noodles could be added, if liked. Menu serves 6.

Peking Jaotzu Dumplings

85 ml (3 fl oz) cold water, plus
  1 tablespoon
350 g (12 oz) plain flour
150 ml (¼ pint) boiling water
225 g (8 oz) lean pork, minced
100 g (4 oz) peeled shrimps, chopped
1 tablespoon minced, peeled root
  ginger
1 tablespoon chopped onion, or
  spring onion
1½ teaspoons salt
1 tablespoon light soy sauce
1 teaspoon sugar
pinch of freshly ground white pepper
pinch of MSG

75 g (3 oz) Chinese cabbage, finely
  shredded

Preparation time: 15 minutes
Cooking time: 3-4 minutes

---

1. Put the 85 ml (3 fl oz) cold water and the flour in a bowl and blend well together. Add the boiling water and mix again. Leave for a few minutes, then knead until smooth.
2. Mix together the pork and shrimps and add the chopped ginger, onion, salt, soy sauce, sugar, pepper, MSG

and tablespoon of water. Add the cabbage to the mixture and beat together into a paste.
3. Roll the dough into a long sausage 4 cm (1½ inch) in diameter. Cut into 4 cm (1½ inch) lengths, form into balls, then roll each one flat into a small pancake disc. Place 1 tablespoon of the stuffing on each pancake. Fold the pancake firmly over the stuffing and press and roll the edges together close to form a half moon.
4. Bring a large pan of water to the boil. Add the dumplings and cook for 3-4 minutes. Drain and serve hot.

Mongolian Lamb in Lettuce Puffs

菜
包
烤
羊
肉

1 kg (2 lb) leg of lamb, boned and
   cut into 3 or 4 pieces
1 tablespoon yellow bean paste
1½ tablespoons soy sauce
2 slices root ginger, peeled and
   shredded
2 garlic cloves, crushed
2 spring onions, shredded
½ teaspoon 5-spice powder
2 tablespoons dry sherry
600 ml (1 pint) vegetable oil
To serve:
lettuce leaves
hoisin sauce

**Preparation time: 15 minutes,
  plus marinating
Cooking time: 1 hour 40
  minutes**

1. Put the lamb pieces into a bowl
with the yellow bean paste, soy sauce,
ginger, garlic, spring onions, 5-spice
powder and sherry. Leave to marinate
for at least 1 hour.
2. Place the lamb in a heatproof
bowl, cover and steam for 1½ hours.
Remove and drain off the liquid.
3. Heat the oil in a wok until it is
smoking, then deep-fry the lamb for
8-10 minutes until crispy. Drain on
paper towels. Cut into 2.5 cm (1 inch)
slices and serve wrapped in an
iceberg lettuce leaf with hoisin sauce.

Left: Mongolian Lamb in Lettuce Puffs
Right: Peking Jaotzu Dumplings
Illustration: Pork butcher with the
tools of his trade.

These savoury stuffed buns are often eaten in China as snacks, on a picnic or while travelling. Here, they could be served as a starter, and a dish of rice or noodles, such as Emerald Fried Rice (page 26), or Northern Fried Noodles (page 44) would be served with the chicken dish. Menu serves 4-6.

Quick-Fried Diced Chicken with Cucumber

450 g (1 lb) chicken breasts,
  skinned and cut into 2.5 cm
  (1 inch) cubes
3 tablespoons cornflour, plus
  3 teaspoons
1 teaspoon salt
2 egg whites, lightly beaten
5½ tablespoons vegetable oil
2 garlic cloves, crushed
3 slices root ginger, shredded
6 tablespoons chicken stock
1 cucumber, cut into 2.5 cm
  (1 inch) cubes
2 tablespoons water
pinch of MSG

Preparation time: 15 minutes
Cooking time: about 5 minutes

1. Dust the chicken cubes with 3 tablespoons cornflour and the salt, then toss in the egg white to coat.
2. Heat 4 tablespoons of the oil in a wok and add the chicken cubes. Stir-fry over heat for about 2 minutes or until the chicken changes colour, then remove from the wok and keep warm.

3. Add the remaining oil to the wok and reheat. When hot, add the garlic and ginger, stir quickly for 15 seconds, then pour in the chicken stock. Remove the ginger and garlic with a perforated spoon. Add the cucumber and return the chicken to the wok. Stir all together to reheat the chicken.
4. Blend the water, remaining cornflour and MSG and add this to the wok to thicken the sauce. Stir for a further 15 seconds then serve on a heated serving dish.

Fried Buns Stuffed with Pork, Prawns and Vegetables

1 tablespoon dried yeast
100 ml (3½ fl oz) warm water
pinch of sugar
450 g (1 lb) plain flour
Filling:
225 g (8 oz) minced pork
100 g (4 oz) peeled prawns, finely
  chopped
200 g (7 oz) Chinese cabbage, finely
  shredded
2 spring onions, finely chopped
2 cm (1 inch) piece root ginger,
  peeled and finely chopped
few drops sesame oil
pinch of MSG
1 tablespoon soy sauce
pinch of freshly ground white pepper
100 ml (3½ fl oz) vegetable oil
watercress and parsley sprigs, to
  garnish

Preparation time: 10 minutes,
  plus proving and rising
Cooking time: 10 minutes

1. Mix the yeast with 2 tablespoons of the warm water and the pinch of sugar. Leave in a warm place until it becomes frothy.
2. Sift the flour into a bowl, add the yeast mixture and the remaining warm water. Knead together to form a soft dough. Continue kneading for about 10 minutes or until the dough becomes smooth and elastic. Place in a bowl and cover with a piece of cling film. Put the bowl in a warm place and leave until the dough has doubled its bulk (about 1 hour).
3. Mix together the pork, prawns, Chinese cabbage, spring onions, ginger, sesame oil, MSG, soy sauce, white pepper and oil in a bowl.
4. When the dough has doubled its bulk, knead it well on a floured board, then return to the bowl and leave it to rise again. When it has again doubled its bulk, knead again for the third time, then roll it into a long sausage. Cut the dough into about 35 pieces and roll each small piece into a ball.
5. Using a rolling pin, roll each ball into a flat circle. Place about 2 teaspoons of filling on the circle of dough and then bring up the edges to form a flower. Twist the edges to-

gether to seal.
6. Heat the wok and put all the prepared buns in it. Pour in about 1½ cups of water and then simmer it for 5-6 minutes. Pour out the water and pour in the oil. Fry the buns for about 3-4 minutes or until the bottoms are golden brown. Remove from the wok and drain on paper towels. Serve immediately, garnished with watercress and parsley.

Top: Fried Buns Stuffed with Pork, Prawns
and Vegetables
Bottom: Quick-Fried Diced Chicken with
Cucumber

The most commonly eaten vegetable in the north is white cabbage. This is a popular way of serving it, which goes well with rich dishes like the Chilli Beef. The addition of the noodles makes this a very filling, satisfying meal. Menu serves 4-6.

Stir-Fried Chilli Beef in Black Bean Sauce

450 g (1 lb) skirt steak, thinly sliced
1 tablespoon soy sauce
1 tablespoon Chinese wine or dry sherry
1 teaspoon sugar
1 teaspoon sesame oil
1 tablespoon cornflour
4 tablespoons vegetable oil
6 tablespoons water
2 tablespoons salted black beans, soaked, rinsed and crushed
1 garlic clove, crushed
1 tablespoon chopped root ginger
2 dried chillis, finely chopped
4 spring onions, cut into 2.5 cm (1 inch) pieces

Preparation time: 10 minutes, plus marinating
Cooking time: about 5 minutes

---

1. In a bowl, mix the slices of beef with the soy sauce, ½ tablespoon wine, ½ teaspoon sugar, the sesame oil, cornflour and 4 tablespoons water. Leave to marinate for 1 hour.
2. Mix together the black beans, remaining sugar, wine and water to form a paste.
3. Heat the wok and pour in the vegetable oil. When it begins to smoke, add the beef and stir-fry until the meat changes colour, then remove with a slotted spoon and keep warm.
4. Stir in the garlic, ginger and chillis. Stir over heat for 30 seconds and then add the black bean paste. Stir together for another 30 seconds, then return the beef and the spring onions to the wok. Toss all together and serve immediately on a warm serving dish.

Northern Fried Noodles

450 g (1 lb) fresh hand-made noodles or egg noodles
4 tablespoons vegetable oil
100 g (4 oz) lean pork, finely shredded
4 dried Chinese mushrooms, soaked for 20 minutes, drained, stemmed and shredded
100-150 g (4-5 oz) Chinese cabbage, finely shredded
3 spring onions, cut into 2.5 cm (1 inch) lengths
1 teaspoon salt
pinch of MSG

2 teaspoons dark soy sauce
1 teaspoon sesame oil

Preparation time: 5 minutes, plus soaking
Cooking time: about 10 minutes

---

1. Bring a large pan of water to the boil, then put in the noodles and bring back to the boil: Remove immediately and drain. Refresh under cold running water and leave to drain again thoroughly.

2. Heat the oil in a wok, then add the pork and mushrooms. Stir-fry over the heat for about 2 minutes, then add the shredded cabbage, spring onions, salt, MSG, and soy sauce.

3. Stir-fry again for about 2 minutes, then add the noodles. Toss together, then add the sesame oil. Mix together so all the ingredients are combined and well heated through.

4. Arrange on a heated serving dish and serve immediately.

Left to right: Northern Fried Noodles, Stir-Fried Chilli Beef in Black Bean Sauce Hot and Sour Cabbage,

Hot and Sour Cabbage

5 tablespoons vegetable oil
3 dried chillis, seeded and finely chopped
½ teaspoon white peppercorns, lightly crushed
1 Chinese cabbage, cut into 4 cm (1½ inch) pieces
2 teaspoons salt
2 tablespoons soy sauce
2 tablespoons sugar
2 tablespoons vinegar
¼ teaspoon sesame oil

Preparation time: 10 minutes
Cooking time: 5 minutes

1. Heat the oil in a wok and add the chillis. Stir for a few seconds, then put in the peppercorns.

2. Raise the heat and add the cabbage. Stir-fry over heat for about 3 minutes, then sprinkle on the salt, soy sauce, sugar, vinegar and sesame oil. Toss all together to mix thoroughly and serve. This dish can also be served cold.

The classic dish from Peking. It is customary in China to serve the soup, made from the duck carcass, at the end of the meal. The pancakes can also be bought ready-made in Chinese super-markets and heated over a steamer. The menu serves 6. Peking Duck is often served also as part of a larger meal, serving 8-10.

Duck Soup

1 duck carcass
1.2 litres (2 pints) cold water
750 g (1½ lb) Chinese cabbage, cut
    into 2.5 cm (1 inch) pieces
1 cake bean curd, cut into 2.5 cm
    (1 inch) squares
1 tablespoon soy sauce
1 tablespoon wine vinegar
pinch of MSG

Preparation time: 10 minutes
Cooking time: About 50
    minutes

1. Put the duck carcass into a pan with cold water and bring to the boil. Simmer for 30 minutes, then remove the carcass.
2. Add the Chinese cabbage, bean curd, soy sauce, vinegar and MSG and bring back to the boil. Simmer for another 10 minutes. Serve hot.

Pancakes

450 g (1 lb) plain flour
250 ml (8 fl oz) boiling water
85 ml (3 fl oz) cold water
1 teaspoon sesame oil

Preparation time: 20 minutes, including resting
Cooking time: about 2 minutes

1. Add the boiling water to the flour and mix well. Add the cold water. Knead the dough thoroughly until it is smooth, then cover and let it rest for 15 minutes.
2. Working on a lightly floured board, divide the dough into 2 pieces and roll each into a long sausage shape, 5 cm (2 inches) in diameter. Cut or pinch into 2.5 cm (1 inch) lengths (altogether about 40 pieces). Flatten each piece with the hand into a pancake shape, keeping cut sides top and bottom. Lightly brush the top surfaces with sesame oil. Stick the pancakes together in pairs, oiled sides inward, then roll out until about 13 cm (5 inches) in diameter.
3. Place a dry crêpe pan or frying pan over medium heat. Cook each pancake on one side until bubbles rise (about 20 seconds), then turn and cook about 10 seconds more on the other side until light brown. Remove from the pan and separate the pancakes quickly, pulling the rounds apart very carefully.
4. Stack the separated pancakes in a pile, oiled sides uppermost, and cover with greaseproof paper. When all are prepared, fold each one into quarters. These pancakes can also be made in advance, stacked, covered in foil and refrigerated. When needed, warm in a steamer until hot, then fold into quarters.

Left to right: Pancakes, Peking Duck, Duck Soup

Peking Duck

1 duck, about 1.5-1.75 kg (3½-4 lb)
½ medium cucumber, cut into matchstick strips
½ bunch spring onions, cut into shreds
Sauce:
2 tablespoons corn oil
1 × 100 g (4 oz) can yellow bean paste
3 tablespoons sugar

Preparation time: 30 minutes, plus drying
Cooking time: 1¼-1½ hours
Oven: 200°C/400°F/Gas Mark 6

1. Wash the duck, dry on paper towels, and hang in a cool airy place (such as a larder or outhouse) to dry the skin for 3 hours or more (preferably overnight).
2. Place the duck on a wire tray over a roasting tin and put into the pre-heated oven on the middle shelf. Roast for 1¼ hours without opening the oven door or basting. At the end of this time, test if the duck is cooked by inserting a skewer in the thickest part of the thigh. If the juices run clear, the duck is ready.
3. Using a small, sharp knife, carve off the skin in small pieces and arrange on a heated serving dish. Carve off the meat in the same way, and arrange separately.
4. Heat the corn oil in a small saucepan until smoking. Add the yellow bean paste and stir over the heat for 2 minutes. Add the sugar and continue to stir over heat for a further 2 minutes. This sauce can be served warm or cold with the Peking duck.
5. Serve the duck skin and meat with the sauce, pancakes, and the shredded cucumber and spring onions. Each guest places a few pieces of skin and meat on a pancake, adds some sauce, spring onion and cucumber shreds, and rolls up the pancake.

The Chinese make extensive use of nuts of all kinds. Here, chicken strips are dipped in chopped walnuts for a really unusual, crunchy-textured dish. Serve rice or noodles to give balance to this high-protein meal. Menu serves 6.

Peking Sliced Fish Pepperpot Soup

醋
椒
魚
片
湯

225 g (8 oz) fish fillets (any firm-fleshed fish will do)
1 tablespoon cornflour
1 egg white, lightly beaten
1½ teaspoons salt
600 ml (1 pint) vegetable oil
900 ml (1½ pints) chicken stock
2 thin slices root ginger, peeled and finely chopped
1 garlic clove, crushed
pinch of MSG
2 tablespoons wine vinegar
½ teaspoon freshly ground white pepper
2 spring onions, finely chopped

Preparation time: 10 minutes
Cooking time: about 5 minutes

1. Cut the fish into 2.5 cm (1 inch) strips. Mix together the cornflour, egg white and a pinch of salt and toss the fish strips in this mixture. Heat the oil in a wok to 180°C/350°F or until a cube of bread browns in 30 seconds. Gently put in the fish strips one by one. Deep-fry for about 1 minute, lift out and drain on paper towels.
2. Heat the stock in a pan and add the ginger, garlic, remaining salt, and MSG. Bring to the boil and simmer for about 1 minute. Add the fish, vinegar and pepper. Simmer for about 3 minutes, then pour into a deep bowl or soup tureen. Sprinkle the soup with the spring onions and serve immediately.

Fried Pork Kidney

炒
腰
花

225 g (8 oz) pigs' kidneys
½ teaspoon salt
1 tablespoon cornflour
4 tablespoons vegetable oil
1 spring onion, finely chopped
1 slice root ginger, peeled and finely chopped
1 garlic clove, crushed
10 g (¼ oz) dried wood ears, soaked for 20 minutes, and drained
50 g (2 oz) bamboo shoots, finely sliced
50 g (2 oz) canned water chestnuts, drained and finely sliced
100 g (4 oz) cabbage, spinach or lettuce, cut into 2.5 cm (1 inch) strips and blanched
1 tablespoon wine vinegar
2 tablespoons soy sauce
1 tablespoon chicken stock

Preparation time: 20 minutes, plus soaking
Cooking time: 5 minutes

1. Split each kidney in half lengthways, and skin and core. Score the surface of each kidney in a diagonal criss-cross pattern, then cut into about 8 pieces. Toss the kidneys with the salt and half the cornflour.
2. Heat 2 tablespoons oil in a wok until smoking, then toss in the kidney pieces. These should quickly curl up to form flowers. Remove with a slotted spoon and keep warm.
3. Heat the remaining oil in the wok and add the spring onion, ginger and garlic. Stir together for a few seconds, then put in the wood ears, bamboo shoots, water chestnuts, cabbage and vinegar. Cook together for 1 minute.
4. Blend the remaining cornflour with the soy sauce and chicken stock. Add to the wok to thicken the sauce. Bring back to the boil and return the kidney flowers to heat through. Serve immediately.

Deep-Fried Chicken with Walnuts

350 g (12 oz) chicken breasts,
skinned and cut into strips
1 egg white
½ teaspoon salt
1 tablespoon white wine
2 tablespoons cornflour
100 g (4 oz) shelled walnuts
300 ml (½ pint) vegetable oil
1 teaspoon salt
1 teaspoon freshly ground white
pepper

**Preparation time: 15 minutes,
plus marinating and soaking
Cooking time: 1-2 minutes**

1. Mix the egg white, salt, wine and cornflour. Toss the chicken in this and leave to marinate for about 10 minutes.
2. Soak the walnuts in boiling water for 10 minutes, then skin and chop finely, or grind.
3. Dip the chicken strips in the chopped walnuts.
4. Heat the oil in a wok until smoking and fry the chicken strips slowly for about 1 minute or until golden brown. Remove and drain on paper towels. Serve on a bed of lettuce leaves, with the mixed salt and pepper as a dip.

Top left: Peking Sliced Fish Pepperpot Soup
Bottom left: Fried Pork Kidney
Below: Deep-Fried Chicken with Walnuts

One of the great delicacies of the Shantung region is Fu Yung Chicken, made by poaching thinly sliced chicken and egg white in oil. Menu serves 6.

Cold Tossed Celery with Mustard Sauce

涼拌芹菜

450 g (1 lb) fresh crisp celery, cut into 4 cm (1½ inch) pieces
2 tablespoons English mustard
250 ml (8 fl oz) water
1 teaspoon salt
pinch of MSG
pinch of sugar
1½ teaspoons cornflour

Preparation time: 5 minutes
Cooking time: about 5 minutes

1. Bring a pan of water to the boil and blanch the celery quickly. Drain and refresh the celery in cold running water and place in the refrigerator to chill.
2. Mix together the English mustard, water, salt, MSG, sugar and cornflour. Bring to the boil and thicken. Remove from the heat and allow to cool. Transfer to a bowl and put into the refrigerator to chill.
3. When ready to serve, pour the sauce over the celery.

Fish Soup

魚

羹

1 large plaice, about 500 g (1¼ lb), skinned and boned
1 dried fish maw (optional)
1.2 litres (2 pints) chicken stock
1 tablespoon Chinese wine or dry sherry
1 teaspoon salt
pinch of MSG
pinch of freshly ground white pepper
2 teaspoons cornflour
1 tablespoon water
2 egg whites
2 spring onions, finely chopped
2 slices cooked ham, shredded

Preparation time: 5 minutes, plus soaking
Cooking time: about 15 minutes

1. Steam the fish fillet until cooked, about 10 minutes. Flake the fish, making sure you remove any bones.
2. Soak the fish maw overnight or until soft, then cut it into small pieces. Heat the stock in a pan and add the flaked fish and the fish maw, together with the wine, salt, MSG and white pepper.
3. Blend the cornflour with the water. When the stock is boiling, stir the cornflour into the stock to thicken it.
4. Beat the egg whites lightly, then pour gently into the boiling stock. Pour into a soup tureen and sprinkle on the finely chopped spring onions and shredded ham.

Fu Yung Sliced Chicken

芙
蓉
鶏

3 chicken breasts, skinned and cut
  into thin slices
50 g (2 oz) cornflour
1.2 litres (2 pints) vegetable oil
10 egg whites, lightly beaten
150 ml (5 fl oz) chicken stock
4 tablespoons frozen peas
¼ teaspoon MSG
½ teaspoon salt
2 teaspoons water

Preparation time: 15 minutes
Cooking time: 5 minutes

Left to right: Fu Yung Sliced Chicken,
Cold-Tossed Celery with Mustard Sauce,
Fish Soup
Illustration: Drawing silk thread.

1. Toss the chicken slices in the cornflour.
2. Heat the oil in a wok. Add the chicken slices and fry for 1½ minutes. Pour in the egg whites in a steady stream and stir. When they rise to the surface, remove the whites and the chicken from the oil with a slotted spoon and drain on paper towels.
3. Put the chicken stock, peas, MSG and salt into a pan and bring to the boil. Blend 1 teaspoon of the remaining cornflour with the water and add to the pan to thicken the sauce. Add the chicken slices and egg and mix gently together with the sauce. Serve immediately.

Peking is known as the mutton city of China. Lamb or mutton, cooked with garlic and spring onion, is served in almost every restaurant there. Menu serves 6-8.

Fish Omelettes

鍋
塌
魚

4 plaice or lemon sole fillets, about 450 g (1 lb), cut into 4 slices
1½ teaspoons salt
1 teaspoon sesame oil
25 g (1 oz) plain flour
2 eggs lightly beaten
2 tablespoons vegetable oil
1 slice root ginger, peeled and finely chopped
1 garlic clove, crushed
2 spring onions, finely chopped
1 tablespoon chicken stock
1 tablespoon Chinese wine or dry sherry

Preparation time: 10 minutes
Cooking time: 10 minutes

1. Sprinkle the fish with salt, sesame oil and plain flour, and dip in egg.
2. Heat 1 tablespoon oil in a frying pan and add the fish. Fry until golden brown. Turn over and add the ginger, garlic and spring onions. Reduce the heat and cover the pan. Add the chicken stock and rice wine and simmer for 5 minutes. Serve hot.

Sautéed Lamb Slices in Garlic Sauce

蒜
泥
羊
肉

450 g (1 lb) lean lamb, sliced very thinly
8 tablespoons vegetable oil
2 tablespoons soy sauce
½ teaspoon salt
1 tablespoon Chinese wine or dry sherry
½ teaspoon Szechuan peppercorns, freshly ground
2 garlic cloves, sliced
225 g (8 oz) spring onions, cut into 4 cm (1½ inch) pieces
1 tablespoon wine vinegar
3 teaspoons sesame oil

Preparation time: 10 minutes, plus marinating
Cooking time: 2-3 minutes

1. Marinate the lamb slices in 2 tablespoons vegetable oil, 1 tablespoon soy sauce, the salt, wine and ground Szechuan peppercorns. Leave to marinate for 15 minutes.
2. Heat the wok and add the remaining oil. When it begins to smoke, drop in the sliced garlic, followed by the lamb. Stir and turn quickly over high heat until the lamb changes colour then place on a heated serving dish with a slotted spoon.
3. Pour off the oil from the wok leaving about 1 tablespoon to coat the bottom. Reheat the wok and add the spring onions, remaining soy sauce, vinegar, and 2 teaspoons of sesame oil. Mix all together over the heat, then return the lamb to the wok. Add the remaining oil and toss together so the lamb is coated in the sauce. Transfer to a warm serving dish and serve immediately.

Below left: Fish Omelettes
Below right: Sautéed Lamb Slices in Garlic Sauce

Above: *Stir-Fried Prawns with Water Chestnuts and Mangetout*
Illustration: Four seasons. Leaf from an album of the Ching Dynasty.

Stir-Fried Prawns with Water Chestnuts and Mangetout

荷豆炒蝦片

450 g (1 lb) uncooked prawns, peeled and deveined
4 tablespoons vegetable oil
3 slices root ginger, peeled
2 tablespoons cornflour, plus 1 teaspoon
1 teaspoon salt
pinch of freshly ground white pepper
1 tablespoon Chinese wine or dry sherry
1 egg white
225 g (8 oz) mangetout, cut in half diagonally
6 canned water chestnuts, drained and cut into thin slices
2 tablespoons water
1 teaspoon sesame oil
2 spring onions, finely chopped

Preparation time: 10 minutes
Cooking time: about 5 minutes

1. Cut the prawns in half lengthways, then wash and dry on paper towels.
2. Heat the oil in a wok until it begins to smoke, then add the slices of ginger to flavour the oil. Remove after 30 seconds.
3. Mix together 2 tablespoons cornflour, the salt, white pepper, wine and egg white in a bowl. Toss the prawns in this mixture. When the prawns are well coated, add them to the hot oil. Turn and stir the prawns until they change colour, then remove from the wok with a slotted spoon.
4. Pour off the oil, leaving about 1 tablespoon to coat the bottom of the wok. Reheat, then add the mangetout and water chestnuts and stir-fry until they change colour. Return the prawns to the wok. Blend the remaining teaspoon of cornflour with the water and stir in to thicken the sauce.
5. When the sauce becomes translucent, add the sesame oil and spring onions. Toss all together and serve immediately.

A *major influence on north-ern cuisine has been the mighty Yellow River, cradle of Chinese civilization, which flows majestically across the North China Plain. Carp from the Yellow River, with golden yellow scales and delicate flesh, is regarded as a particular delicacy. Menu serves 6-8.*

Yellow River Carp

1 carp, about 900 g (2 lb)
2 teaspoons salt
1½ tablespoons plain flour
1½ tablespoons cornflour
5 tablespoons water
600 ml (1 pint) vegetable oil
2 tablespoons lard
Sauce:
2 tablespoons sugar
4 tablespoons wine vinegar
1 tablespoon soy sauce
2 tablespoons Chinese wine or dry sherry
6 tablespoons water
1 tablespoon cornflour

Preparation time: 15 minutes
Cooking time: about 10 minutes

1. Rub the carp inside and out with salt. Score on both sides with shallow criss-cross cuts. Blend the flour and cornflour with the water to make a batter. Turn the fish in the batter until well coated on both sides.
2. Heat the oil in a wok until smoking. Lower the fish in a wire basket into the oil and fry for 7-8 minutes. Remove, drain and keep hot.
3. Melt the lard in a pan, then add all the sauce ingredients. Stir together over medium heat for 2 minutes until the sauce becomes thick and translucent. Transfer the fish to a heated serving dish and pour the sauce over.

Clockwise from the front: Peking Sliced Chicken Omelettes in Garlic and Onion Sauce, Yellow River Carp, Hot Shallow-Fried King Prawns
Illustration: Fishing with trained cormorants.

Hot Shallow-Fried King Prawns

4 tablespoons vegetable oil
2 slices root ginger, peeled and finely chopped
2 spring onions, finely chopped
1 garlic clove, crushed
450 g (1 lb) uncooked king prawns, peeled and deveined
1½ tablespoons tomato ketchup
2 tablespoons chicken stock
3 tablespoons sugar
1 tablespoon sherry

Preparation time: 10 minutes
Cooking time: about 5 minutes

1. Heat the oil in a wok until it is smoking. Add the ginger, half of the spring onions and the garlic. Toss together, then add the prawns. Continue to stir-fry for about 2 minutes, then remove from the wok and drain on paper towels.
2. Add the tomato ketchup, chicken stock, sugar and sherry. Bring to the boil over high heat and boil to reduce by one-third. Return the prawns and simmer for about 2 minutes. Sprinkle on the remaining spring onions and serve on a bed of lettuce leaves.

Peking Sliced Chicken Omelettes in Garlic and Onion Sauce

3 chicken breasts, skinned and each cut into 4 slices
1 teaspoon salt
pinch of freshly ground white pepper
2 eggs, beaten
3 tablespoons vegetable oil
2 garlic cloves, thinly sliced
2 spring onions, finely chopped
4 tablespoons chicken stock
2 tablespoons wine vinegar
pinch of MSG

Preparation time: 10 minutes
Cooking time: 5 minutes

1. Rub the chicken slices with a pinch of salt and pepper, then turn in the beaten eggs until well coated.
2. Heat the oil in a wok until smoking, then add the chicken pieces one by one. Reduce the heat to low and fry for 1½ minutes, then turn the slices over to cook on the other side. After 30 seconds, sprinkle on the garlic, spring onions, chicken stock, remaining salt, vinegar and MSG. Leave to simmer for 2 minutes.
3. Remove the chicken slices and cut if liked into smaller pieces. Place on a heated serving dish and pour the sauce over the chicken.

Tomatoes are plentiful in Peking during the summer and are often cooked with beef. Menu serves 6-8.

Fish in Vinegar Sauce

 2 tablespoons vegetable oil
3 spring onions, white part only, cut into 2.5 cm (1 inch) sections
450 g (1 lb) white fish fillets, each fillet cut in half
2 tablespoons Chinese wine or dry sherry
2 tablespoons soy sauce
3 tablespoons wine vinegar
150 ml (¼ pint) chicken stock
1 teaspoon chopped root ginger
2 tablespoons sugar
2 teaspoons cornflour
1 teaspoon sesame oil

Preparation time: 10 minutes
Cooking time: 15 minutes

1. Heat the oil in a wok and add the spring onions. Stir-fry until golden, then add the fish and wine and cook until all the wine evaporates.
2. Add the soy sauce, half the vinegar, the chicken stock, ginger and half the sugar. Bring to the boil, then simmer for 5 minutes.
3. Mix the remaining sugar with the remaining vinegar and the cornflour. Stir into the wok and thicken the sauce. Sprinkle on the sesame oil just before serving.

Deep-Fried Chicken Pieces

6 chicken joints, skinned and cut into pieces
2 spring onions, finely chopped
3 thin slices root ginger
2 pieces star anise
3 tablespoons soy sauce
1 tablespoon cornflour
1 egg white
600 ml (1 pint) vegetable oil
sesame oil, for sprinkling
1½ teaspoons salt
1 teaspoon pepper

Preparation time: 15 minutes, plus seasoning
Cooking time: 5-6 minutes

1. Place the chicken pieces in a bowl with the spring onions, ginger, star anise, soy sauce, cornflour and egg white. Mix all together thoroughly and leave to season for about 1 hour.
2. Heat the oil in a wok to 180°C/350°F, or until a cube of bread browns in 30 seconds, and put in the chicken pieces. Fry for about 3 minutes, then remove and drain. Reheat the oil and fry the chicken pieces again until brown. Remove and drain thoroughly on paper towels. Arrange on a serving dish and sprinkle with sesame oil.
3. Mix together the salt and pepper and use as a dip for the chicken pieces.

Red-Cooked Beef with Tomatoes

番
茄
牛
肉

1.5 kg (3 lb) shin beef
3 tablespoons vegetable oil
2 large onions, peeled and thinly
   sliced
2 slices root ginger, peeled and
   shredded
2 garlic cloves, crushed
1 piece dried tangerine peel, soaked
   for 20 minutes and drained
1 teaspoon salt
5 tablespoons soy sauce
450 g (1 lb) tomatoes, skinned and
   chopped
1 tablespoon sugar
6 tablespoons Chinese wine or dry
   sherry
½ tablespoon hoisin sauce
tomato slices, to garnish
1 tablespoon finely chopped chives, to
   garnish

Preparation time: 15 minutes
Cooking time: about 3½ hours

1. Put the beef in a pan with enough water to cover, bring to the boil and boil for 10 minutes. Drain the beef, reserving the liquid, and cut into 4 cm (1½ inch) cubes.
2. Heat the vegetable oil in a heavy pan, add the meat and stir-fry over high heat for 5-6 minutes. Remove the beef and drain on paper towels.
3. Add the onions, ginger and garlic to the pan and stir-fry over medium heat for 3-4 minutes. Measure the boiling liquid and make up to 750 ml (1½ pints) with hot water, if necessary. Add to the pan with the tangerine peel, salt and 2 tablespoons soy sauce. Bring to the boil then add the beef cubes. Bring the pan back to the boil, then reduce the heat to low, cover and simmer gently for 2 hours.
4. Add the tomatoes to the pan together with the remaining soy sauce, and the sugar, sherry and hoisin sauce. Stir well, cover and continue cooking over a very low heat for another hour. Garnish with tomato slices, sprinkling with the chopped chives just before serving.

Top left: Deep-Fried Chicken Pieces
Bottom left: Fish in Vinegar Sauce
Right: Red-Cooked Beef with Tomatoes
Illustration: Making wine from wild rice or millet.

These elegant desserts could be served with any of the menus. In China, sweet dishes like these might well be served at the start of the meal.

Steamed Pears in Syrup

225 g (8 oz) flaked rice
25 g (1 oz) almonds, skinned and
    roughly chopped
1 × 100 g (4 oz) can lotus seeds,
    drained and roughly chopped
6 red and green glacé cherries, finely
    chopped
50 ml (2 fl oz) vegetable oil
2 tablespoons sugar
4 pears, peeled and cored
Sauce:
1 tablespoon sugar
100 ml (3½ fl oz) water
25 g (1 oz) cornflour
few drops of red food colouring

Preparation time: 10 minutes
Cooking time: 45 minutes

1. Cover the flaked rice with water and steam for 30 minutes.
2. Mix together the cooked rice, almonds, lotus seeds, cherries, vegetable oil and sugar.
3. To make the sauce, dissolve the sugar in the water. Blend the cornflour with the food colouring and add this to the sugar and water. Bring to the boil to form a sauce.
4. Stuff the rice mixture into the pear cores. Place in a steamer basket and steam for about 15 minutes.
5. Serve the pears with the sauce poured over.

Top: Peking Brittle Glazed Toffee Apples
Bottom: Steamed Pears in Syrup
Illustration: Northern mountains.

Peking Brittle Glazed Toffee Apples

100 g (4 oz) flour
1 egg
100 ml (3½ fl oz) water, plus
    2 tablespoons
4 crisp apples, peeled, cored, and cut
    into 12 wedges
600 ml (1 pint) vegetable oil, plus
    1 tablespoon
6 tablespoons sugar
2 tablespoons water
3 tablespoons golden syrup

Preparation time: 15 minutes
Cooking time: 10 minutes

1. Mix together the flour, egg and water to make a batter. Dip each piece of apple into the batter.
2. In a wok, heat 600 ml (1 pint) oil to 180°C/350°F or until a cube of bread browns in 30 seconds. Deep-fry the apple pieces for 2 minutes, then remove and drain on paper towels.
3. In another pan, heat together the sugar, and remaining vegetable oil and water. Dissolve the sugar over gentle heat, then simmer for 5 minutes, stirring constantly. Add the syrup and boil until the hard crack stage is reached (151°C/340°F) or until it forms brittle threads when dropped into iced water. Put in the fried apples and turn to coat each piece.
4. Remove the apple pieces with a slotted spoon and drop into iced water. Remove immediately and serve.

Meringue Balls with Bean Paste Stuffing

Meringue Balls with Bean Paste Stuffing

高
力
豆
沙

1 × 225 g (8 oz) can red bean paste
6 egg whites
pinch of cornflour
100 g (4 oz) plain flour, plus extra
   for dusting
300 ml (½ pint) vegetable oil
2 tablespoons sugar

Preparation time: 15 minutes
Cooking time: about 3-4
   minutes

1. Make 20 small balls with the red bean paste, using about 2 teaspoons of paste for each ball.
2. Beat the egg whites to form stiff peaks. Fold in the pinch of cornflour and plain flour.
3. Dust the prepared bean paste balls with plain flour, then coat well with beaten egg white.
4. Heat the vegetable oil in a wok, then put in the coated red bean paste balls and fry gently until golden brown and puffed up. Drain on kitchen paper and sprinkle with sugar. Serve immediately.

東部：上海

Eastern China lies on the great plain formed by the river delta of the mighty Yangtse River, which flows into the sea just north of Shanghai. This is one of China's leading agricultural regions, for the river delta contains some of the most fertile land in China, farmed for some 2000 years, and it was from the produce of this region that much of the classical cooking of China was created.

Both wheat and rice are grown here, as well as barley, corn, soy beans and an abundance of vegetables. Peanuts produce the oil which is largely used in cooking. The Yangtse is the greatest rice-producing region in China, and it follows that all rice-based products exist in abundance – among them rice wine, used extensively in dishes. Rice is often used too as a stuffing – or to make such classic dishes as Eight Treasure Rice – a sweet steamed pudding, made of glutinous rice and steamed with glacé fruits, bean paste, and nuts. Chekiang province, south of the Yangtse, is known as the land of rice and fish, and it is one of the wealthiest and most heavily populated regions of China. This area of the lower Yangtse is well-irrigated, criss-crossed with innumerable streams, ponds and lakes, ideal for ducks, fish, frogs and eels. Hence such classic dishes as the duck dishes of Nanking and the freshwater fish and shellfish dishes of Yangchow. Leaves of the lotus, another natural product of the ponds, streams and lakes, are frequently used for wrapping food for cooking (usually by steaming). Meat, chicken, savoury rice and whole fish are cooked in this way. During cooking, the contents of the package become imbued with the aromatic flavour of the lotus leaves. East China is also well known for paper-wrapped dishes – morsels of chicken, beef, prawns etc, flavoured with mushrooms, ginger, onions etc are wrapped up in little packets of cellophane paper. The packets are deep-fried in hot oil and opened with chopsticks.

Shanghai, on the Yangtse estuary, is the largest city in China, and one of the most cosmopolitan, being the centre of China's trade and industry. Its cuisine is noted for its use of red-cooking, with dark soy sauce, and its lavish use of sugar, which produces rich, sweet dishes with exquisite flavours and appearance.

A well-balanced meal to serve with rice. The dark sweet sauce served with the Long-Braised Soy Beef is typical of this region — the people of East China have a reputation for being sweet-toothed. Menu serves 4.

Mussel and Bean Curd Soup

1 kg (2 lb) mussels, washed and scrubbed
1 tablespoon vegetable oil
2 spring onions, finely sliced
900 ml (1½ pints) chicken stock
2 cakes bean curd, cut into small dice
1 × 200 g (7 oz) can straw mushrooms, drained and cut in half
2 leaves Chinese cabbage, blanched and shredded
large pinch of freshly ground white pepper

1 teaspoon salt
large pinch of MSG
3 teaspoons cornflour
2 tablespoons water
few drops of sesame oil

Preparation time: 20 minutes
Cooking time: 20 minutes

1. Place the mussels in a pan with a little water, put on the lid and boil hard until the shells have opened, shaking the pan from time to time. Remove the mussels from the shells and reserve. Discard unopened shells.
2. Heat the oil in a wok, add the spring onions and stir-fry gently for a few seconds. Add the chicken stock, bean curd, mussels, straw mushrooms, Chinese cabbage, white pepper, salt, and MSG. Simmer gently for 5 minutes. Blend the cornflour with the water and stir into the soup to thicken it. Pour into a tureen and drizzle on a few drops of sesame oil just before serving.

Stir-Fried Beansprouts with Green Peppers

3 tablespoons vegetable oil
3 slices root ginger, peeled
1 large green pepper, cored, seeded
    and cut into shreds
450 g (1 lb) beansprouts
1 teaspoon salt
1 tablespoon cider vinegar
1 teaspoon sesame oil
pinch of MSG
1 teaspoon cornflour
1 tablespoon water
1 tablespoon shredded spring onions

Preparation time: 15 minutes
Cooking time: 10 minutes

1. Heat the vegetable oil in a wok. Add the slices of ginger. Fry the ginger for 1 minute, then discard.
2. Add the green pepper and then the beansprouts. Stir-fry together for a few minutes. When the colour begins to change, stir in the salt, vinegar, sesame oil and MSG. Blend cornflour and water and stir into the wok.
3. When the beansprouts are coated with the glaze, add the spring onions. Toss all together, then transfer to a serving dish. Serve hot.

Left: *Mussel and Bean Curd Soup*
Right: Top, *Stir-Fried Beansprouts with Green Peppers.* Bottom: *Long-Braised Soy Beef*
Illustration: Dipping porcelain plates in wet sand before firing.

Long-Braised Soy Beef

450 g (1 lb) shin of beef, cut into
    2.5 cm (1 inch) cubes
4 tablespoons dark soy sauce
2 tablespoons Chinese wine or dry
    sherry
500 ml (18 fl oz) cold water
2 tablespoons sugar
3 slices root ginger, peeled
3 pieces star anise
25 g (1 oz) dried wood ears, soaked
    for 20 minutes, and drained

Preparation time: 5 minutes,
    plus soaking
Cooking time: about 3 hours

1. Place the beef cubes, soy sauce and Chinese wine in a pan. Bring to the boil, then add the water, sugar, ginger and star anise. Cover and simmer for about 2½ hours, or until tender.
2. Add the wood ears and simmer for another 30 minutes. Add more water if the sauce seems too dry or thick.
3. Transfer the meat to a serving dish along with the wood ears and pour the sauce over (the sauce should be quite thick and syrupy).

Yangchow Fried Rice is substantial enough to be eaten on its own. Together these dishes will serve 4-6, with the colourful soup as a starter.

Steamed Trout in Black Bean Sauce

豆
豉
魚

1 trout, about 1 kg (2¼ lb)
1 teaspoon salt
½ teaspoon freshly ground white pepper
½ teaspoon ground ginger
2 spring onions, shredded
2 cm (¾ inch) piece root ginger, peeled and shredded
3 tablespoons vegetable oil
1 tablespoon salted black beans, soaked, drained and crushed
2 small dried chillis, finely chopped
2 tablespoons light soy sauce
1 tablespoon Chinese wine or dry sherry
½ teaspoon sugar
1 teaspoon sesame oil

Preparation time: 10 minutes, plus soaking
Cooking time: about 30 minutes
---

1. Wash the fish and pat dry with paper towels. With a sharp knife, score the fish on both sides with diagonal, parallel cuts. Rub in a mixture of salt, white pepper and ground ginger, both on the inside and the outside. Lay the fish on a heatproof dish and sprinkle over half the shredded spring onions and ginger.
2. Heat 2 tablespoons of the oil in a wok. Add the black beans and half the chillis and stir-fry together for a few seconds. Add half the soy sauce, the Chinese wine and sugar to the wok and cook together for 1 minute.
3. Pour the sauce slowly over the fish. Place the fish, in its heatproof dish, in a steamer and steam for about 20 minutes. Test to see if the fish is cooked by inserting a chopstick into the flesh. If it is soft, then the fish is cooked. Carefully remove the cooked spring onions, ginger and chillis and sprinkle the remaining ones on top of the fish. Add the rest of the soy sauce and the sesame oil. Spoon the sauce that has collected in the bottom of the dish over the fish and serve hot.

Coral Cabbage

珊
瑚
白
菜

4 tablespoons vegetable oil
1½ tablespoons dried shrimps, soaked for 20 minutes and drained
1 tablespoon winter pickle
1 kg (2¼ lb) Chinese cabbage, roughly shredded
salt
freshly ground white pepper
3 tablespoons red bean curd cheese
3 tablespoons tomato purée
1 tablespoon light soy sauce
25 g (1 oz) butter
100 ml (3½ fl oz) chicken stock

Preparation time: 10 minutes, plus soaking
Cooking time: 30-35 minutes
Oven: 180°C, 350°F, Gas Mark 4

1. Heat the oil in a wok, then add the shrimps and pickle. Turn in the oil a few times, then add all the cabbage and sprinkle it with salt and pepper.
2. Turn the cabbage in the oil for 2-3 minutes until it is well coated.
3. Mix together the bean curd, tomato purée and soy sauce and add to the cabbage. Turn until well coated, then transfer to a casserole.
4. Dot the top of the cabbage with butter, pour the stock on top and cover. Place the casserole in a preheated oven and cook for 25 minutes.

Yangchow Fried Rice

揚
州
炒
飯

5 tablespoons vegetable oil
2 medium onions, peeled and finely sliced
2 slices root ginger, peeled and diced
100 g (4 oz) minced pork
salt
1 tablespoon light soy sauce
1 teaspoon sugar
500 g (1¼ lb) cooked rice
2 eggs, lightly beaten
2 tablespoons cooked green peas
2 tomatoes, chopped
3 dried Chinese mushrooms, soaked for 20 minutes, drained, stemmed and chopped
freshly ground black pepper

Preparation time: 20 minutes, plus soaking
Cooking time: about 10 minutes

1. Heat half the oil in a large wok or frying pan. Add the onions and ginger, and stir-fry for 1 minute. Add the minced pork and stir-fry for 3 minutes. Add ½ teaspoon salt, soy sauce and sugar and stir-fry for 1 minute.
2. Add the rice to the wok to heat through, turning and stirring well.
3. Heat the remaining oil in another wok. Season the beaten egg with salt and pepper and add to the wok. Stir and turn the eggs gently. As soon as they have set, add the peas, tomatoes and mushrooms.
4. Stir for about 1 minute, then turn the egg mixture into the wok containing the rice. Mix lightly together, then serve in a heated bowl.

Wonton Soup with Watercress

西
洋
菜
餛
飩
湯

1 large bunch watercress
225 g (8 oz) minced pork
1 tablespoon soy sauce
2 pinches of MSG
2 teaspoons sesame oil
pinch of sugar
1 tablespoon Chinese wine or dry sherry
pinch of freshly ground white pepper
1 teaspoon ground ginger
1.2 litres (2 pints) chicken stock
1 teaspoon salt
100 g (4 oz) ready-made wonton skins

Preparation time: 20 minutes
Cooking time: 20 minutes

1. Divide the watercress into two bunches. Chop one bunch finely and cut the other in half.
2. In a bowl, mix together the minced pork, finely chopped watercress, soy sauce, 1 pinch of MSG, 1 teaspoon sesame oil, sugar, cooking wine, white pepper and ginger. Beat well to combine thoroughly.
3. Place about 1 heaped teaspoon of the filling in the middle of a ready-made wonton skin, gather up the corners to completely enclose the meat, then twist the top to close tightly. Continue until all the meat mixture is used up.
4. In a deep saucepan, heat the chicken stock with the salt and a pinch of MSG.
5. In a separate pan, bring about 1.5 litres (2½ pints) of water to the boil. When boiling furiously, drop in the wontons. Reduce the heat and simmer the wontons for about 5 minutes. Drain the wontons and place in a deep bowl. Line soup bowls with the remaining watercress. Put in the wontons. Pour on the chicken stock, sprinkle with the remaining sesame oil and serve hot.

Clockwise from the right: Wonton Soup with Watercress, Yangchow Fried Rice, Steamed Trout in Black Bean Sauce, Coral Cabbage

An ideal late after-theatre supper. The ingredients for these dishes can mostly be chopped and sliced in advance. Marrows and pumpkins are produced in abundance in this region. As well as being used for soup, they are often used as containers for meat stuffings or whole chickens, which are then steamed. Menu serves 4-6.

Stir-Fried Courgettes with Button Mushrooms

5 tablespoons vegetable oil
1 teaspoon salt
½ teaspoon freshly ground white
    pepper
100 g (4 oz) button mushrooms,
    sliced
100 g (4 oz) courgettes, sliced into
    3 mm (⅛ inch) rings
pinch of MSG

Preparation time: 10 minutes
Cooking time: 5 minutes

1. Heat 4 tablespoons of the oil in a wok. Add the salt, pepper and mushrooms and stir-fry for about 2 minutes, or until the mushrooms change colour. Transfer the mushrooms to a hot serving dish and wipe the wok clean with paper towels.
2. Heat the wok again and add the remaining tablespoon of oil. Add the sliced courgettes and stir-fry for one minute. Put the mushrooms back into the wok and toss together for 30 seconds. Sprinkle on the MSG, pour into a hot serving dish and serve immediately.

Dried Shrimp and Marrow Soup

1.75 litres (3 pints) chicken stock
50 g (2 oz) dried shrimps, soaked for
    20 minutes, and drained
50 g (2 oz) peeled prawns, chopped
50 g (2 oz) dried Chinese
    mushrooms, soaked for
    20 minutes, drained, stemmed
    and cubed
100 g (4 oz) canned straw
    mushrooms, drained
1 small marrow, about 750 g
    (1½ lb), cubed
100 g (4 oz) lean pork, cubed
1 slice cooked ham, 2.5 cm (1 inch)
    thick, cubed
5 cm (2 inch) piece canned bamboo
    shoot, cubed
50 g (2 oz) crab meat, cubed
2 teaspoons salt
large pinch of MSG
few drops of Chinese wine or dry
    sherry
few drops of sesame oil

large pinch of freshly ground white
    pepper
2 eggs
2 spring onions, finely chopped

Preparation time: 10 minutes,
    plus soaking
Cooking time: 20 minutes

1. Heat the chicken stock in a large pan and add the shrimps, prawns, Chinese mushrooms, straw mushrooms, marrow, pork, ham, bamboo shoot, and crab meat. Bring to the boil and simmer for 5 minutes.
2. Add the salt, MSG, Chinese wine, sesame oil, and white pepper.
3. Beat the eggs, then pour them slowly into the soup. Pour into a soup tureen and sprinkle with the spring onions.

Chicken with Bamboo Shoots

竹
ル
芍
鸡

225 g (8 oz) chicken breasts,
    skinned and finely sliced
salt
freshly ground white pepper
2 teaspoons Chinese wine or dry
    sherry
2 egg whites
50 g (2 oz) cornflour
300 ml (½ pint) vegetable oil
100 ml (3½ oz) chicken stock, plus
    1 tablespoon
pinch of sugar
2 slices cooked ham, thinly shredded
100 g (4 oz) canned bamboo shoots,
    drained, sliced and blanched
75 g (3 oz) mangetout, washed and
    dried
few drops of sesame oil
coriander sprigs, to garnish

Preparation time: 20 minutes
Cooking time: 15 minutes

1. Put the sliced chicken breasts into a bowl and mix together with 1 teaspoon salt, pinch of white pepper, 1 teaspoon Chinese wine, egg whites, and three-quarters of the cornflour. Blend thoroughly.
2. Heat the vegetable oil in a wok to 180°C/350°F or until a cube of bread browns in 30 seconds. Add the chicken slices and stir in the hot oil, separating the slices gently. After about 2 minutes lift out the chicken and drain on paper towels. Keep warm.
3. Pour off most of the oil, leaving just enough to coat the bottom of the wok, then reheat. Pour in the chicken stock, remaining wine, sugar and shredded ham. Season with salt and pepper to taste and then put the chicken back into the wok along with the bamboo shoots and mangetout.
4. Mix the remaining cornflour with the tablespoon of chicken stock and stir this into the wok. Bring to the boil and simmer until it thickens, then sprinkle on the sesame oil. Toss all together and serve immediately, garnished with coriander.

Clockwise from the bottom: Dried Shrimp and Marrow Soup, Stir-Fried Courgettes with Button Mushrooms, Chicken with Bamboo Shoots

A hearty, filling meal. Serve with plenty of rice or noodles, together with a fresh-tasting vegetable dish such as stir-fried mangetout or beansprouts, to balance the buns and the meat. In China these buns are often served on their own as a snack. The Knuckle of Pork with its rich, glossy, sugar-glazed sauce is another example of the dark, sweet dishes of this region. Serves 6-8.

Shanghai Long-Cooked Knuckle of Pork

1 knuckle of pork, about 2 kg
   (4½ lb)
3 spring onions, cut into 2.5 cm
   (1 inch) lengths
6 tablespoons dark soy sauce
40 g (1½ oz) caster sugar
6 tablespoons Chinese wine or dry
   sherry
4 slices root ginger, peeled
25 g (1 oz) lard

Preparation time: 5 minutes
Cooking time: 2½ hours

1. Score the pork skin all over with a sharp knife.
2. Place the knuckle of pork in a heavy pan or casserole and cover with water. Bring to the boil and simmer for 10 minutes. Skim and simmer for another 15 minutes. Skim again, then pour off one-third of the broth.
3. Add the spring onions, soy sauce, sugar, sherry, ginger and lard to the remaining broth. Cover and simmer for 2 hours, turning the pork every 30 minutes. By the end of the cooking time, the liquid in the pan should have reduced by a quarter. Lift out the knuckle of pork and place on a warmed serving dish.
4. Turn the heat up high to reduce the sauce even further, until it becomes rich and glossy. Pour over the knuckle of pork and serve immediately with plain vegetables and rice.

Chicken, Asparagus and Straw Mushroom Soup

2 chicken breasts, about 175 g
   (6 oz), skinned and thinly sliced
1 egg, beaten
1 tablespoon cornflour
150 ml (¼ pint) vegetable oil
1.2 litres (2 pints) chicken stock
8 canned asparagus spears, cut into
   2 cm (¾ inch) pieces
8-10 canned straw mushrooms,
   drained and sliced in half
½ teaspoon salt
pinch of MSG
½ teaspoon sesame oil

Preparation time: 15 minutes
Cooking time: 10 minutes

1. Place the chicken slices in a bowl with the egg and cornflour and turn until evenly coated.
2. Heat the oil in a wok and add the chicken slices. Stir-fry gently for about 1 minute, then remove from the oil and drain. Pour off the oil and add the stock to the wok. Heat until boiling, then add the chicken slices, asparagus and straw mushrooms. Finally add the salt, MSG, and sesame oil. Bring back to the boil and serve.

Paotzu Steamed Buns Stuffed with Crab Meat, Pork and Cabbage

2 teaspoons dried yeast
1 teaspoon sugar
300 ml (½ pint) warm water
450 g (1 lb) plain flour
350 g (12 oz) minced pork
50 g (2 oz) crab meat, flaked
225 g (8 oz) Chinese cabbage, finely
   shredded, blanched and drained
1 teaspoon salt
2 tablespoons soy sauce
1 teaspoon freshly ground white
   pepper
pinch of MSG
1 teaspoon sesame oil
2 spring onions, finely sliced
2 cm (1 inch) piece root ginger,
   peeled and finely chopped

Preparation time: 20 minutes,
**   plus rising**
Cooking time: 20 minutes

1. Sprinkle the yeast and sugar on to the warm water and leave in a warm place until it becomes frothy. Sift the flour, then stir the yeast mixture into the flour. Knead together until smooth, cover and leave in a warm place until it has doubled its bulk (at least 1 hour). Knead again and then let it rest in a warm place for 30 minutes, covered.
2. Mix the minced pork, crab meat and cabbage together. Add the salt, soy sauce, white pepper, MSG, sesame oil, spring onions and ginger. Mix together thoroughly.
3. Knead the dough for the third time, then roll out into 2 long sausage shapes. Cut each 'sausage' into 16-18 pieces. Flatten each piece into a round with the palm of the hand. Place some of the pork and crab meat mixture in the centre and gather dough up over the filling and twist to seal. Leave the buns in a warm place to rise. When they are twice their original size place in a steamer basket and steam vigorously for 20 minutes. Serve hot.

Any leftover buns can be reheated for a snack, either by steaming for 5 minutes or shallow-frying in a little oil for 5-6 minutes.

Top to bottom: Shanghai Long-Cooked Knuckle of Pork, Chicken, Asparagus and Straw Mushroom Soup, Paotzu Steamed Buns Stuffed with Crab Meat, Pork and Cabbage

Chinese meals are often balanced with both a meat and a fish dish. Serves 4, or would serve 6 if accompanied by a substantial rice dish such as Yangchow Fried Rice (page 67) or Shanghai Vegetable Rice with Chinese Sausages (page 77).

Bean Curd Soup

1.5 litres (2½ pints) chicken stock
6 dried Chinese mushrooms, soaked for 20 minutes, drained and stemmed
3 cakes bean curd, cut into 1 cm (½ inch) squares
50 g (2 oz) canned bamboo shoots, drained and sliced
50 g (2 oz) uncooked prawns, peeled
200 g (7 oz) cooked pork, finely sliced
3 slices root ginger, peeled
pinch of salt
pinch of freshly ground white pepper
1 spring onion, finely chopped
pinch of MSG
½ teaspoon sesame oil

Preparation time: 10 minutes, plus soaking
Cooking time: 45 minutes

1. Put the chicken stock in a large pan and bring to the boil.

2. Cut the mushrooms into bite-sized pieces and add to the pan with the bean curd and bamboo shoots. Bring back to the boil.
3. Simmer for about 30 minutes. Cut the prawns into bite-sized pieces and add together with the pork slices,

Top: Clear-Simmered Meatballs
Bottom: Bean Curd Soup

ginger, salt and pepper. Cook for another minute until the prawns change colour. Sprinkle on spring onions, MSG and sesame oil. Serve hot.

Clear-Simmered Meatballs

750 g (1½ lb) minced pork
50 g (2 oz) dried Chinese mushrooms, soaked for 20 minutes, drained, stemmed and diced
100 g (4 oz) canned bamboo shoots, drained and diced
100 g (4 oz) dried shrimps, soaked for 20 minutes, drained and diced
2 spring onions, finely chopped
2.5 cm (1 inch) piece root ginger, peeled and finely chopped
1 egg
2 tablespoons cornflour
2 tablespoons salt
600 ml (1 pint) vegetable oil, plus 4 tablespoons

1 teaspoon sesame oil
5 tablespoons chicken stock
1 tablespoon soy sauce

Preparation time: 10 minutes plus soaking
Cooking time: 25 minutes

1. In a bowl, mix together the pork, mushrooms, bamboo shoots, shrimps, spring onions, ginger, egg, 1½ tablespoons cornflour, salt, 4 tablespoons vegetable oil and the sesame oil. Mix together thoroughly and form into balls, using about 1 tablespoon mixture per ball.

2. Heat the remaining oil in a wok until it is smoking, then add the meatballs. Fry until brown on the outside. Remove with a slotted spoon and drain on paper towels.
3. Pour off the oil. Add the chicken stock to the wok and return the meatballs. Bring to the boil, then simmer for about 10 minutes. Lift out the meatballs, drain and place on a warmed serving dish.
4. Add the soy sauce to the wok. Mix the remaining cornflour with the remaining tablespoon of chicken stock, add to the wok and stir until the sauce thickens. Pour the sauce over the meatballs and serve immediately.

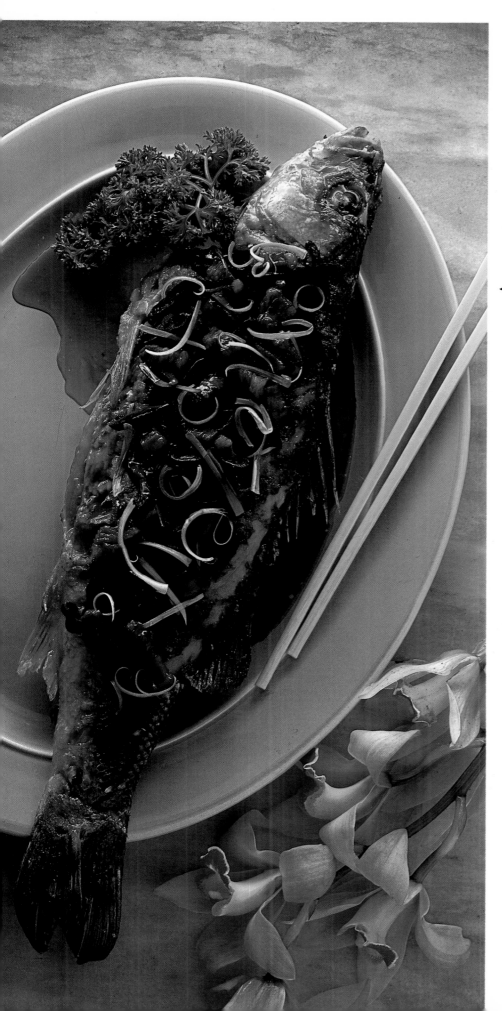

Crispy Whole Fish in Shredded Pork and Mushroom Sauce

脆
皮
魚

1 carp, trout or sea bass, about 1 kg (2 lb)
2 teaspoons salt
25 g (1 oz) cornflour
600 ml (1 pint) vegetable oil
100 g (4 oz) belly of pork, finely shredded
3 slices root ginger, peeled and shredded
6 large dried Chinese mushrooms, soaked for 20 minutes, drained, stemmed and shredded
3 spring onions, shredded
2½ tablespoons soy sauce
1 tablespoon sugar
3 tablespoons chicken stock
3 tablespoons Chinese wine or dry sherry
1 garlic clove, crushed
1 dried chilli, finely chopped
parsley sprig, to garnish

Preparation time: 10 minutes, plus soaking and seasoning
Cooking time: about 20 minutes

1. Rub the fish with salt and corn-flour inside and out. Leave to season for 1 hour at least.
2. Heat the oil in a wok to 180°C/ 350°F, or until a cube of bread browns in 30 seconds. Add the fish and fry for 5-6 minutes, turning over twice during this time. Remove the fish and drain.
3. Pour off the oil from the wok, leaving about 1 tablespoon in the bottom. Add the pork and shredded ginger and stir-fry together for about 2 minutes. Add the mushrooms and spring onions and continue to stir-fry for another 2 minutes, then add the soy sauce, sugar, chicken stock, wine, garlic and chilli. Bring to the boil, then return the fish to the wok. Baste it with the boiling sauce and spoon over the mushrooms and pork.
4. Simmer on both sides for about 2 minutes, then lift the fish onto a serving dish. Spoon the sauce over the fish and pile the pork and mushrooms on top of the fish. Garnish with parsley sprig.

Crispy Whole Fish in Shredded Pork and Mushroom Sauce

The people of the Lower Yangtse are fond of sharp-tasting food, such as the Salt and Pepper Prawns, which is served with mild flavoured dishes such as the chicken and the rice. Rice Congee is a kind of gruel, often eaten as a snack, or for breakfast. Menu serves 6.

Salt and Pepper Prawns

4 tablespoons vegetable oil
450 g (1 lb) uncooked prawns, peeled and deveined
2 spring onions, cut into 2.5 cm (1 inch) pieces
1 garlic clove, crushed
2 small chillis, sliced into long shreds
2 pieces star anise
¼ teaspoon freshly ground white pepper
½ teaspoon Szechuan peppercorns, freshly ground
¾ teaspoon salt

Preparation time: 10 minutes
Cooking time: 5 minutes

1. Heat the oil in a wok. Add the prawns and stir-fry for about 1½ minutes. Remove the prawns and drain on paper towels. Pour off all but 1 tablespoon of the oil.
2. Add the other ingredients except the salt and pepper. Stir-fry for two seconds, then return the prawns to the wok. Add salt and pepper and stir. Turn out onto a heated serving dish. This is very good served as a starter.

Clockwise from the top: Stir-Fried Chicken Slices with Mangetout, Salt and Pepper Prawns, chicken Rice Congee
Illustration: Travelling fruit sellers.

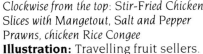

Stir-Fried Chicken Slices with Mangetout

450 g (1 lb) chicken breasts, skinned and cut into thin slices
salt
pinch of freshly ground white pepper
pinch of MSG
4 tablespoons vegetable oil, plus 1 teaspoon
1 teaspoon cornflour
1 egg white
225 g (8 oz) mangetout, stringed and cut in half on a slant
25 g (1 oz) petits pois
1 teaspoon sesame oil

Preparation time: 15 minutes, plus marinating
Cooking time: 7-8 minutes

1. Marinate the chicken breast slices in the mixed ½ teaspoon salt, white pepper, MSG, 1 teaspoon vegetable oil, cornflour, and egg white for 30 minutes.
2. Heat 1 tablespoon of cooking oil in a wok. Drop in the mangetout with a pinch of salt and stir-fry until they are cooked slightly yet still crunchy. Transfer to a warmed serving dish and reheat the wok.
3. Add the remaining vegetable oil, and when hot add the chicken slices. Separate the slices, and stir-fry gently until the chicken slices change to a white colour. Drop in the petits pois and stir all together for about 1 minute. Take the wok off the heat and stir in the teaspoon of sesame oil. Toss together and then arrange on the serving dish. Serve immediately.

Chicken Rice Congee (Soft Rice)

1.75 litres (3 pints) chicken stock
100 g (4 oz) pudding rice, washed and drained
salt
freshly ground white pepper
2 egg whites, lightly beaten
100 g (4 oz) chicken breast meat, skinned and finely minced
To garnish:
2 slices of ham, finely minced
2 spring onions, finely chopped

Preparation time: 15 minutes
Cooking time: 2 hours

1. Pour the chicken stock into a large pan and bring to the boil. Stir in the washed rice while still boiling and then reduce the heat so the stock is just simmering. Let the stock and rice simmer for about 2 hours with the lid on, stirring occasionally. Add salt and pepper to taste.
2. When ready to serve, mix the egg whites with the chicken meat and stir into the rice gruel. Serve immediately. The heat from the congee will cook the chicken without any further cooking being needed. Spoon the congee into bowls, and sprinkle the minced ham and spring onions on top, to garnish.

An ideal menu for those who like highly spiced food. The Smoked Fish Slices (fresh fish marinated and spiced to taste like smoked fish) make a delicious, unusual hors d'oeuvre, while the strong-tasting Stewed Pork Flavoured with Dried Squid dish is offset by the vegetable rice to make a substantial meal. Serves 6.

Smoked Fish Slices

450 g (1 lb) cod fillet or any other firm white fish, cut into matchbox-sized pieces
3 tablespoons soy sauce
2 tablespoons Chinese wine or dry sherry
pinch of salt
3 spring onions, finely chopped
2 slices root ginger, peeled and finely chopped
250 ml (8 fl oz) water
50 g (2 oz) sugar
½ teaspoon 5-spice powder
600 ml (1 pint) vegetable oil

Preparation time: 15 minutes, plus marinating
Cooking time: 25-30 minutes

1. Marinate the fish in soy sauce, wine and salt for about 1 hour.
2. Remove the fish from the marinade and drain. Pour the marinade into a pan and bring to the boil. Add the spring onions and ginger, together with the water, sugar and 5-spice powder. Simmer until reduced by half, then strain the sauce through a sieve into a bowl.
3. Heat the oil in a wok to 180°C/350°F, or until a cube of bread browns in 30 seconds. Drop in a few pieces of fish at a time. Fry for about 4 minutes or until crisp and golden brown. Remove the fish pieces from the oil, drain on paper towels, then put into the sauce for about 5 minutes. Remove the fish pieces from the sauce and allow to cool on a plate. Serve cold as an hors d'oeuvre.

Stewed Pork Flavoured with Dried Squid

50 g (2 oz) dried squid
1 teaspoon bicarbonate of soda
1 kg (2 lb) lean belly of pork, cut
    into 2.5 cm (1 inch) cubes
3 tablespoons dark soy sauce
3 tablespoons Chinese wine or dry
    sherry
1 tablespoon sugar
pinch of freshly ground white pepper
pinch of salt
100 ml (3½ fl oz) cold water
2 slices root ginger, peeled

15 g (½ oz) dried wood ears, soaked
    for 20 minutes and drained

Preparation time: 5 minutes,
plus soaking and marinating
Cooking time: 1½ hours

1. Place the dried squid in enough water to cover, add the bicarbonate of soda and leave to soak for 1 hour. Rinse and drain.

2. Place the belly pork in a bowl with the soy sauce, wine, sugar, white pepper and salt and marinate for 10 minutes.

3. Put the pork, squid and marinade into a pan and bring to the boil. Add the water and ginger root and simmer gently for about 1 hour, or until tender. Add the dried wood ears and another 2 tablespoons of water and bring back to the boil. Simmer for a further 30 minutes and serve hot.

Shanghai Vegetable Rice with Chinese Sausages

225 g (8 oz) long-grain rice, washed
    under running water
350 ml (12 fl oz) water
225 g (8 oz) Chinese sausages, cut
    into 1 cm (½ inch) chunks
3 tablespoons lard or vegetable oil
2 teaspoons salt
3 slices root ginger, peeled
750 g (1½ lb) spring greens,
    washed and cut into 2.5 cm (1
    inch) pieces
pinch of MSG

Preparation time: 10 minutes
Cooking time: 30 minutes

1. Put the rice into a large pan with the water. Bring to the boil, then reduce the heat and add the Chinese sausages. Bring back to the boil again, stirring all the time, and then cover and simmer over low heat for 10 minutes.

2. Heat the lard or oil in a wok. Add 1 teaspoon of salt to the wok and the 3 slices of ginger, then put in the spring greens. Stir-fry until the spring greens change colour and then remove from the wok and stir into the rice. Add the remaining salt and the MSG to the rice and cover to steam for another 20 minutes.

Left: Smoked Fish Slices
Right: Stewed Pork Flavoured with Dried Squid, Shanghai Vegetable Rice with Chinese Sausages

An elegant party menu. The fish is a little fiddly to prepare, but well worth the trouble. Serve the duck first, as a starter to be eaten with the fingers. Noodles or rice should be served with this and a light pudding such as Almond Float (page 104) would end the meal nicely. Menu serves 5-6.

White Butterfly Fish Soup

1 small sea bass, about 750 g
  (1½ lb), cleaned and filleted, with
  skin still on
600 ml (1 pint) vegetable oil
100 g (4 oz) rice noodles
100 ml (3½ fl oz) water
225 g (8 oz) watercress, washed, cut
  roughly in half, and blanched
1.75 litres (3 pints) chicken stock
large pinch of MSG
½ teaspoon salt
large pinch of freshly ground white
  pepper
1 tablespoon Chinese wine or dry
  sherry

2 spring onions, finely chopped

Preparation time: 30 minutes
Cooking time: 25 minutes

---

1. Lie the fish fillet with the skin on the board. Hold the knife at a 45° angle and cut a slice which stops before it cuts through the skin. Make the next cut about 5 mm (¼ inch) away at the same angle but cut right through the skin. What you should have now is a slice of fish with a deep cut dividing it almost in half. Continue until all the fish is sliced up.

2. Heat the oil in a wok until it reaches 180°C/350°F, or until a cube of bread browns in 30 seconds, then plunge the rice noodles into the hot oil. They should immediately puff up. Remove them from the oil and drain on paper towels.

3. Pour off the oil from the wok leaving just enough to coat the bottom. Put the water into the wok and heat it until simmering. Gently put the butterflies in separately and remove them when the become opaque in colour. Carefully rinse them in cold water to stop any further cooking.

4. Arrange the blanched watercress in the bottom of a deep soup tureen. Put the rice noodles on top, and then arrange the butterflies on top.

5. Heat the chicken stock in a wok. Flavour it with MSG, salt, white pepper and Chinese wine. When ready to serve the soup, pour the boiling stock on top of the arranged fish and sprinkle with the finely chopped spring onions.

Deep-Fried Boneless Duck

生
炸
去
骨
鸭

1 duck, about 1.5 kg (3½ lb),
  washed and dried
1 egg
3 tablespoons cornflour
2 tablespoons self-raising flour
3 pieces star anise
600 ml (1 pint) vegetable oil
Master sauce:
450 ml (¾ pint) chicken stock
150 ml (¼ pint) light soy sauce
4 garlic cloves, crushed
1 tablespoon sugar
2 teaspoons 5-spice powder
To serve:
lettuce leaves
hoisin sauce

Preparation time: 5 minutes
Cooking time: about 1 hour

1. Parboil the duck in a large pan of water for about 5 minutes, then remove and drain.
2. Mix together the egg, cornflour, and self-raising flour to form a batter.
3. Mix together the ingredients for the Master sauce and the star anise in a deep casserole over medium heat. Add the duck and coat it in the sauce. Leave the duck to simmer in the sauce for about 40 minutes, turning it every 10 minutes.
4. Remove the duck and drain off the sauce thoroughly. When cool enough, remove all the bones from the duck and divide it into 8 pieces. Place the duck pieces in the batter and turn until evenly coated.
5. Heat the oil in a wok to 180°C/ 350°F or until a cube of bread browns in 30 seconds. Deep-fry the duck pieces for about 7-8 minutes, then remove from the oil and drain thoroughly on paper towels. Cut the duck into bite-sized pieces and arrange on a serving dish. The duck can be wrapped in crisp lettuce leaves and served with hoisin sauce.

To make spring onion flowers, trim both ends so that the stalk measures 7.5 cm (3 inches). Using a very sharp knife, finely shred the green end to within 2.5 cm (1 inch) of the stem. Leave in iced water for 1 hour to allow them to open.

Left: *White Butterfly Fish Soup*
Right: *Deep-Fried Boneless Duck*

Illustration: 'Dreaming of enlightenment in a thatched cottage.'

An unusual, colourful menu for a special occasion. If glutinous rice is unavailable, use pudding rice instead for the Steamed Pearl Balls. Serves 4.

Pork Chop Noodle Soup

225 g (8 oz) egg noodles
450 g (1 lb) thinly sliced pork chops, cut into 5 cm (2 inch) squares and pounded with a meat mallet
1 teaspoon chopped spring onions
2 tablespoons soy sauce
2 teaspoons sugar
2 tablespoons Chinese wine or dry sherry
1 teaspoon cornflour
pinch of freshly ground white pepper
5 tablespoons vegetable oil
1.2 litres (2 pints) chicken stock
salt
1 bunch watercress
2 spring onions, cut into 2.5 cm (1 inch) lengths
pinch of MSG

Preparation time: 20 minutes, plus marinading
Cooking time: 30 minutes

---

1. Blanch the noodles in boiling water, then drain and refresh in cold water.
2. Place the meat in a bowl with the spring onions, 1 tablespoon soy sauce, 1 teaspoon sugar, 1 tablespoon wine, cornflour and white pepper. Mix well and leave to marinate for 30 minutes.
3. Heat 4 tablespoons of the oil in a wok. Add the pork and stir-fry until both sides are golden brown. Remove and drain. Pour off the oil.
4. Bring the chicken stock to the boil in a large pan. Add salt to taste and then drop in the blanched noodles and watercress. Bring back to the boil, then pour into a large heated serving bowl, or individual soup bowls.
5. Heat the remaining oil in the wok and add the spring onions, remaining wine, soy sauce, sugar and the MSG. Stir-fry for 2 minutes. Pile the pork on top of the noodles and add the sauce.

Clockwise from the bottom: Pork Chop Noodle Soup, Watercress and Water Chestnut Salad, Steamed Pearl Balls over Chinese Mushrooms

Steamed Pearl Balls over Chinese Mushrooms

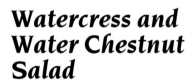

12 dried Chinese mushrooms, soaked for 20 minutes in 150 ml (¼ pint) warm water
1 chicken stock cube
225 g (8 oz) minced pork
100 g (4 oz) canned water chestnuts, drained and finely chopped
1 egg white
1 tablespoon Chinese wine or dry sherry
pinch of salt
pinch of freshly ground white pepper
1 teaspoon MSG
225 g (8 oz) glutinous rice, soaked for 30 minutes, and drained
1 teaspoon cornflour
2 teaspoons water
parsley sprigs, to garnish

Preparation time: 15 minutes, plus soaking
Cooking: about 1 hour

Watercress and Water Chestnut Salad

2 bunches watercress, washed, blanched and finely chopped
8 canned water chestnuts, drained
3 teaspoons soy sauce
3 teaspoons sesame oil
pinch of salt
1 teaspoon sugar
tomato slices, to garnish

Preparation time: 10 minutes

---

1. Place the chopped watercress and water chestnuts in a large salad bowl.
2. Mix together the soy sauce, sesame oil, salt and sugar. Sprinkle onto the watercress and chestnuts and toss together thoroughly. Chill and serve, garnished with sliced tomato.

1. Drain the mushrooms, reserving the soaking liquid. Remove the stems and return the mushrooms to the liquid together with the chicken stock cube. Bring to the boil and simmer for 20 minutes until the mushrooms are soft.
2. Mix the minced pork with the water chestnuts, egg white, wine, salt, white pepper, and MSG. Make meatballs about the size of a walnut and roll them in the soaked rice until coated.
3. Drain the mushrooms and use them to line a lightly greased bowl. Fill the bowl with the meatballs, on top of the mushrooms. Place the bowl in a steamer over boiling water and steam for about 30 minutes.
4. Pour any excess liquid from the bowl into a pan over medium heat. Blend the cornflour with the 2 teaspoons water and stir into the pan until the sauce thickens. Pour the sauce over the bowl and garnish with parsley sprigs. Serve from the bowl.

Illustration: Detail from 18th century Chinese wallpaper.

Lotus leaves are frequently used to wrap food for cooking (like foil). During the long steaming process the contents of the package become imbued with the aromatic flavour of the dried lotus leaves. The packages are brought to the table and each person unwraps his own, eating the contents from the leaves with chopsticks (the leaves are then discarded). Menu serves 4.

Cold Spiced French Beans

荷葉絲蒸肉

225 g (8 oz) French beans
1½ teaspoons salt
2.5 cm (1 inch) piece root ginger, peeled and finely chopped
1 dried chilli, finely chopped
1 teaspoon Szechuan or black peppercorns
2 tablespoons sesame oil
1 dried chilli, finely chopped
25 g (1 oz) sugar
2 tablespoons wine vinegar

Preparation time: 15 minutes, plus soaking and chilling
Cooking time: 10 minutes

1. Top and tail the beans, string them, then cut in half. Blanch the beans and refresh under cold, running water. Add the salt and leave them to soak in a large bowl for 20 minutes.
2. Drain the beans and arrange on a serving dish. Mix the ginger and chilli together in a bowl.
3. Heat the wok and dry-fry the Szechuan peppercorns until fragrant. Pour in the sesame oil, then the chopped dried chilli, sugar and vinegar, and fry together for 30 seconds. Pour the hot mixture over the ginger and chilli, mix together and pour over the beans. Toss well, then chill before serving.

Steamed Ground Rice and Pork Wrapped in Lotus Leaves

荷
葉
粉
蒸
肉

450 g (1 lb) belly of pork, cut into
    4 pieces
1 tablespoon light soy sauce
600 ml (1 pint) vegetable oil
6 tablespoons rice powder
1 teaspoon 5-spice powder
1 garlic clove, crushed
3 spring onions, finely chopped
3 slices root ginger, peeled and finely
    chopped
1 teaspoon sugar
pinch of salt
pinch of MSG
3 tablespoons oyster sauce
2 teaspoons sesame oil
4 dried lotus leaves, soaked for
    20 minutes, and drained

Preparation time: 15 minutes,
    plus soaking
Cooking time: about 3 hours

1. Put the pieces of belly pork into a pan of water and bring to the boil. Simmer for about 10-15 minutes, then lift out the pork, drain and dry on paper towels.

2. Rub the pork skin with soy sauce. Heat the oil in a wok to 180°C/350°F or until a cube of bread browns in 30 seconds and then put in the pork pieces. Deep-fry for about 5 minutes or until the skin is crunchy and crisp. Remove from the oil and drain.

3. Cut the fried pork into 1 cm (½ inch) pieces. Put the pork pieces into a bowl along with the rice powder, 5-spice powder, garlic, spring onions, ginger, sugar, salt, MSG, and oyster sauce. Mix together thoroughly. Sprinkle on the sesame oil and mix in.

4. Place a quarter of the mixture on each of the lotus leaves, wrap up tightly and tie with string. Place the parcels in a steamer basket and steam for about 2½ hours.

Left: Cold Spiced French Beans
Right: Steamed Ground Rice and Pork Wrapped in Lotus Leaves

The Miniature Chops make a good starter. Rice and salad go well with the dumplings to form the bulk of this meal. Menu serves 6.

Egg Dumplings with Transparent Noodles and Fried Bean Curd

50 g (2 oz) minced pork
2 teaspoons soy sauce
1 tablespoon Chinese wine or dry
     sherry
pinch of freshly ground white pepper
2 teaspoons sesame oil
½ teaspoon cornflour
1.25 litres (2¼ pints) water
½ packet of fried bean curd cubes,
     halved
50 g (2 oz) pea starch noodles,
     soaked for 5 minutes, and drained
pinch of salt
pinch of MSG
2 eggs, beaten
1 spring onion, finely chopped

**Preparation time: 10 minutes,
     plus soaking
Cooking time: 30 minutes**

1. Mix the minced pork with 1 teaspoon soy sauce, the wine, white pepper, 1 teaspoon sesame oil and the cornflour.
2. Bring the water to the boil in a deep saucepan. Drop in the bean curd and noodles, along with the salt, MSG, remaining soy sauce and sesame oil. Bring to the boil and simmer gently for 10 minutes.
3. Heat an oiled crêpe pan. Place 1 tablespoon of beaten egg in the pan to make a small, round, thin pancake about 6 cm (2½ inches) in diameter. Put 1 teaspoon of the minced pork mixture onto the pancake and then fold in half to form a dumpling. Cook the dumplings over low heat until lightly browned on both sides.
4. Drop the dumplings into the soup and bring to the boil. Turn down the heat and simmer for about 10 minutes. Add the chopped spring onion just before serving.

Crispy Three-Spiced Miniature Chops

香脆小排骨

1 kg (2¼ lb) lamb chops, cut into
   2.5-4 cm (1-1½ inch) piece
1 teaspoon salt
1 tablespoon curry powder
1 cm (½ inch) piece root ginger,
   peeled and chopped
1 egg, beaten
25 g (1 oz) cornflour
600 ml (1 pint) vegetable oil
2 chillis, shredded
1 garlic clove, crushed
salt
freshly ground white pepper

Preparation time: 20 minutes
Cooking time: about 5 minutes

1. Place the lamb pieces in a bowl. Mix the salt, curry powder and half the chopped ginger together, and rub the lamb pieces with this mixture. Add the egg and the cornflour to the bowl and toss the pieces well.
2. Heat the oil in a wok until smoking, and put in the chops one at a time. Turn them over in the oil for 3-4 minutes then lift out and drain on paper towels.
3. Pour off the oil from the wok, leaving enough to coat the bottom, and reheat. Add the chillis, remaining ginger, garlic, large pinch of salt, and white pepper. Stir together for 30 seconds, then return the chops to the wok. Sprinkle the wok again with a large pinch of salt and pepper. Turn and toss again for a further 30 seconds and serve.

Use a heavy chopping board and a Chinese cleaver to cut the lamb chops. Cut each chop through the bone into 2-3 pieces.

Left: Egg Dumplings with Transparent Noodles and Fried Bean Curd. Right: Crispy Three-Spiced Miniature Chops

The duck is served whole and pulled apart with chopsticks at the table to be eaten with rice and the yams. Menu serves 6.

Shanghai Hoisin Duck Cooked with Yams

1 duck, about 1.5 kg (3½ lb), washed and dried
1 teaspoon salt
1 teaspoon freshly ground white pepper.
1 tablespoon hoisin sauce
3 tablespoons Chinese wine or dry sherry
3 spring onions, finely chopped
6 slices root ginger, peeled
450 g (1 lb) small yams, washed, peeled and cut into 2.5 cm (1 inch) chunks

Preparation time: 10 minutes
Cooking time: 2½ hours
Oven: 200°C, 400°F, Gas Mark 6; then 180°C, 350°F, Gas Mark 4

1. Rub the dry duck with salt and pepper and leave for 2 hours.
2. Place the duck on a rack in an ovenproof dish and put in the preheated oven. Roast for 15 minutes on each side until the oil starts to seep out of the duck and both sides are lightly browned.
3. Pour off the oil, then brush the duck all over with the hoisin sauce and also brush inside the body cavity. Place the wine, spring onions, ginger slices and yams in the body cavity. Cover the dish completely with foil and turn down the oven. Roast for 1 hour.
4. After 1 hour, baste the duck with the pan juices, reseal the foil and cook for another hour. The duck should now be ready. Test by inserting a skewer into the meatiest part of the leg. If the juices run clear, the duck is cooked. If the juices have some blood in them, the duck needs further cooking. The duck should be tender enough to be pulled apart easily. Serve with the yams and rice.

Spiced Beansprouts with Cucumber Shreds

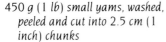

1 kg (2¼ lb) beansprouts
½ cucumber, cut into shreds
50 g (2 oz) dried shrimps, soaked for 20 minutes, and drained
Sauce:
1 teaspoon soy sauce
1 teaspoon salt
1 teaspoon wine vinegar
1½ teaspoons sesame oil
½ teaspoon sugar
pinch of MSG

Preparation time: 10 minutes, plus soaking
Cooking time: 10 minutes

1. Place the beansprouts in a pan, pour over enough boiling water to cover, then drain. Place the shredded cucumber on a serving dish and pile the beansprouts on top. Sprinkle with the dried shrimps.
2. Mix together the sauce ingredients and pour over the vegetables just before serving.

Top: Shanghai Hoisin Duck Cooked with Yams

Bottom: Spiced Beansprouts with Cucumber Shreds

Three Shredded and Five Ingredients Soup

1.5 litres (2½ pints) chicken stock
1 chicken stock cube
15 g (½ oz) root ginger, peeled and chopped
2 garlic cloves, crushed
25 g (1 oz) onion, chopped
25 g (1 oz) dried Chinese mushrooms, soaked for 20 minutes, drained, stemmed and chopped
25 g (1 oz) dried shrimps, soaked for 20 minutes, drained and chopped
2 spring onions, shredded
3 large peeled prawns, shredded
100 g (4 oz) Chinese cabbage, finely shredded
1 teaspoon sesame oil

Preparation time: 10 minutes, plus soaking
Cooking time: 20 minutes

1. Heat the stock in a wok until boiling and dissolve the stock cube.
2. Add the ginger, garlic, onion, mushrooms and shrimps and simmer for 5 minutes.
3. Adjust the seasonings, then add the shredded spring onions, prawns and cabbage and allow to simmer for a further 2 minutes. Sprinkle on the sesame oil and serve immediately.

Below: Three Shredded and Five Ingredients Soup
Illustration: Painting designs on porcelain.

The Blanched Prawns could be served with the dip as a starter. This menu serves 6, with rice.

Red-Cooked Pork with Wood Ears and Bamboo Shoots

木耳竹笋红烧肉

750 g (1½ lb) lean belly of pork, cut into 2 cm (¾ inch) cubes
3 tablespoons Chinese wine or dry sherry
3 tablespoons dark soy sauce
1½ tablespoons sugar
½ teaspoon freshly ground white pepper
3 slices root ginger, peeled
6 tablespoons water
50 g (2 oz) dried wood ears, soaked for 20 minutes, and drained
100 g (4 oz) canned bamboo shoots, drained and cut into bite-sized pieces

Preparation time: 10 minutes, plus soaking
Cooking time: about 1½ hours

1. Place the pork in a pan and add the wine, soy sauce, sugar and pepper. Stir well, add the ginger and water and bring to the boil.
2. Cover tightly and simmer for about 1½ hours, or until meat is tender. After 1 hour's cooking, add the wood ears and bamboo shoots. Serve with rice or pancakes.

Fish Rolls

魚丸

4 dried Chinese mushrooms, soaked for 20 minutes, drained, stemmed and sliced thinly
5 cm (2 inch) piece canned bamboo shoot, cut into shreds
2 slices cooked ham, cut into shreds
100 g (4 oz) peeled prawns, finely minced
1 spring onion, finely chopped
pinch of MSG
pinch of salt
pinch of freshly ground white pepper
450 g (1 lb) plaice fillets, cut into thin, flat, slices
pinch of plain flour, plus extra for dusting
6 egg whites
pinch of cornflour
1.2 litres (2 pints) vegetable oil

Preparation time: 20 minutes, plus soaking
Cooking time: 4-5 minutes

Blanched Prawns in Ginger Dip

1. Mix together the Chinese mushrooms, bamboo shoot, ham, prawns, spring onion, MSG, salt and white pepper.

2. Place an equal amount of the mixture on each plaice slice and roll up firmly. Dust lightly with plain flour.

3. Beat the egg whites until stiff, then add a pinch each of plain flour and cornflour. Fold in gently.

4. Heat the oil in a wok to 180°C/350°F or until a cube of bread browns in 30 seconds. Dip each fish roll in the egg white, making sure it is coated completely, then gently lower into the oil. Fry until golden brown all over. Lift out the fish rolls and drain on paper towels. Serve immediately, on a lettuce leaf.

清煮鮮蝦

1 litre (1¾ pints) water
450 g (1 lb) uncooked prawns,
   peeled and deveined
Dip sauce:
1 tablespoon shredded root ginger
1 tablespoon shredded spring onion
3 tablespoons vegetable oil
1 garlic clove, lightly crushed
2 tablespoons soy sauce
1 tablespoon Chinese wine or dry
   sherry
pinch of sugar
pinch of MSG

Preparation time: 5 minutes
Cooking time: 10 minutes

1. Put the water into a pan and bring to the boil. Drop in the prawns. Wait until they change colour, then remove immediately and drain. Transfer to a serving dish and serve with the Dip sauce.

2. Put the shredded ginger and spring onions into a bowl. Heat the vegetable oil over high heat until it smokes, and then drop in the garlic to flavour the oil. Leave for about 1 minute, then discard the garlic. Pour the boiling oil onto the ginger and spring onions, and add the soy sauce, Chinese wine, sugar, and MSG.

For these Chinese prawn dishes you need the large, uncooked prawns which are usually sold frozen in their shells. Chinese supermarkets sell them frozen in large packs.

Left to right: Red-Cooked Pork with Wood Ears and Bamboo Shoots, Fish Rolls, Blanched Prawns in Ginger Dip

Squirrel Fish is so called because the body of the fish, when placed in the hot oil, curls up to resemble a squirrel's tail. Serve the chicken legs on their own, as a starter, and serve rice with the fish. Menu serves 4-6.

Deep-Fried Chicken Legs

6 chicken drumsticks
225 g (8 oz) minced pork
50 g (2 oz) canned water chestnuts, finely chopped
1 tablespoon Chinese wine or dry sherry
½ teaspoon salt
1 teaspoon sugar
1 teaspoon freshly ground white pepper
2.5 cm (1 inch) piece root ginger, peeled and finely chopped
2 spring onions, finely chopped
1 egg

1 teaspoon sesame oil
25 g (1 oz) cornflour
450 ml (¾ pint) vegetable oil
Batter:
1 egg
50 g (2 oz) plain flour
50 g (2 oz) cornflour

Preparation time: 20 minutes
Cooking time: 5 minutes

1. Without breaking the skin, push and scrape back the meat off the chicken drumsticks at the end of the leg, leaving the meat and skin still attached to the bone at the knuckle.

2. Mix together the minced pork and finely chopped water chestnuts. Add the wine, salt, sugar, white pepper, ginger, spring onions, egg, sesame oil and cornflour. Make sure this is thoroughly blended together. Shape about 1 tablespoon of this mixture on to the bone of each drumstick, pressing it on firmly. Carefully turn the chicken meat and skin back over the minced pork mixture, covering it completely.

3. To make the batter, mix the egg, plain flour and cornflour together. Add enough cold water to thin out the mixture and make a smooth consistency.

4. Heat the oil in a wok to 180°C/350°F or until a cube of bread browns in 30 seconds. Dip the stuffed chicken legs into the batter, then lower them into the oil. Deep-fry gently until golden brown and cooked through, about 5 minutes. Remove from the oil and drain on paper towels. Serve hot.

Bean Curd, Cha Tsai and Dried Shrimp Soup

25 g (1 oz) dried shrimps, soaked for 20 minutes
1.75 litres (3 pints) chicken stock
1 tablespoon Chinese wine or dry sherry
25 g (1 oz) Szechuan pickle (cha tsai), thinly sliced
1 teaspoon salt
2 cakes bean curd, cut into 1 cm (½ inch) squares
1 spring onion, finely chopped
½ teaspoon sesame oil
pinch of MSG

Preparation time: 10 minutes, plus soaking
Cooking time: 25 minutes

Left to right: Deep-Fried Chicken Legs, Squirrel Fish, Bean Curd, Cha Tsai and Dried Shrimp Soup

1. Drain the shrimps and reserve the soaking liquid.
2. Add the liquid from the shrimps to the stock with the wine and bring to the boil.
3. Add the sliced pickle and dried shrimps and simmer for 10 minutes. Add the bean curd and salt and bring to the boil again.
4. Add the spring onions, sesame oil and MSG and serve immediately.

To remove the backbone easily, open out the gutted fish and lay, skin side up, on a board. Press down hard along the backbone with the heel of your hand, then turn the fish over. The backbone should now lift out quite easily, using a sharp knife.

Squirrel Fish

1 sea bass, carp or bream, about 750 g (1½ lb)
½ teaspoon salt
1 tablespoon Chinese wine or dry sherry
600 ml (1 pint) vegetable oil
3 tablespoons cornflour
Sauce:
1 slice root ginger, shredded
2 garlic cloves, finely chopped
1 small onion, peeled and diced
1 carrot, peeled and diced
6 dried Chinese mushrooms, soaked for 20 minutes, drained, stemmed and shredded
6 canned water chestnuts, diced
50 g (2 oz) frozen peas, defrosted
6 tablespoons chicken stock
2 tablespoons sugar
2 tablespoons wine vinegar
4 tablespoons tomato ketchup
1 tablespoon dark soy sauce
1 teaspoon cornflour
2 tablespoons water
1 teaspoon sesame oil

Preparation time: 45 minutes, plus soaking and marinating
Cooking time: about 12 minutes

1. Split the fish in half, leaving the head and skin whole. Remove the backbone. Place the fish skin side down on a board and score the flesh with diagonal crisscross cuts, almost down to the skin (do not cut through the skin). Rub the fish with salt and wine and marinate for 10 minutes.
2. Heat the oil in a wok to 180°C/350°F or until a cube of bread browns in 30 seconds. Coat the fish with the cornflour, then place in the hot oil and deep-fry for 5-6 minutes. Remove and drain on paper towels.
3. Reheat the oil, return the fish to the wok and deep-fry for another 1-2 minutes. Remove and drain.
4. Pour off all but 2 tablespoons of oil from the wok and reheat. Add the ginger and garlic and stir-fry for a few seconds. Add the onion and carrot and stir-fry for 1 minute then add the mushrooms, water chestnuts and peas and cook for another minute. Stir in the stock, sugar, vinegar, ketchup, soy sauce and the cornflour blended with the water. Bring to the boil and stir until the sauce thickens, then add the sesame oil. Place on a serving dish and pour the sauce over.

The Cold Bean Curd dish is served as a starter. Lion's Head Meatballs is a classic dish which is often served with noodles draped over to represent the 'mane'. Serves 4.

Stir-Fried Broad Beans with Pickled Cabbage and Spring Onions

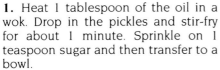

2½ tablespoons vegetable oil
100 g (4 oz) pickled mustard greens, chopped
1½ teaspoons sugar
450 g (1 lb) frozen broad beans, parboiled and shells removed
3 spring onions, finely chopped
pinch of salt
pinch of freshly ground white pepper

Preparation time: 15 minutes
Cooking time: 5 minutes

1. Heat 1 tablespoon of the oil in a wok. Drop in the pickles and stir-fry for about 1 minute. Sprinkle on 1 teaspoon sugar and then transfer to a bowl.
2. Wipe the wok clean with paper towels and reheat again. Add the remaining oil and stir-fry the broad beans and spring onions with the salt, pepper and remaining sugar.
3. Stir-fry until the colour changes, then return the pickles to the wok, stir well together, and then transfer to a warm serving dish. This dish can be served hot or cold.

Cold Bean Curd with Cha Tsai and Dried Shrimps

Top: Stir-Fried Broad Beans with Pickled Cabbage and Spring Onions

Bottom: Cold Bean Curd with Cha Tsai and Dried Shrimps

---

1 cake bean curd, cut into 1 cm (½ inch) squares
1 tablespoon Szechuan pickle (cha tsai), chopped
1 tablespoon dried shrimps, soaked for 20 minutes and drained
1 spring onion, finely chopped
½ teaspoon salt
1 tablespoon soy sauce

½ teaspoon sugar
1 tablespoon sesame oil

Preparation time: 5 minutes, plus soaking

1. Put the bean curd in the bottom of a serving dish. Mix the chopped pickle

and shrimps with the spring onion and sprinkle over the top.
2. Mix the salt, soy sauce, sugar and sesame oil together in a bowl and toss the other ingredients in this just before serving.

Right: Lion's Head Meatballs
Illustration: winnowing rice.

Lion's Head Meatballs

獅
子
頭

1 kg (2¼ lb) minced pork
4 tablespoons soy sauce
1 tablespoon Chinese wine or dry
  sherry
1½ tablespoons sugar
1 cm (½ inch) piece root ginger,
  peeled and finely chopped
½ teaspoon freshly ground black
  pepper
1 tablespoon sesame oil
4 tablespoons vegetable oil
500 ml (18 fl oz) cold water
1 tablespoon cornflour
2 tablespoons cold water

Preparation time: 20 minutes
Cooking time: about 3½ hours

1. In a bowl mix together the pork,
1 tablespoon soy sauce, wine, ½ tablespoon sugar, ginger, pepper and

sesame oil until everything is thoroughly blended. Beat well, then form
into 4 equal-sized meatballs.
2. Heat a wok, then add 4 tablespoons vegetable oil. Add the meatballs and brown thoroughly all over.
Put the water into a pan and bring to
the boil. Gently transfer the meatballs
to the pan, add the remaining soy
sauce and sugar, cover and simmer
gently for about 3 hours, checking
from time to time to see that the
liquid has not all evaporated.
3. After 3 hours, the meatballs
should be ready. Lift out the meatballs, drain and place on a serving
dish. Keep warm while you thicken
the sauce by stirring in the blended
cornflour and water. When thickened,
pour the sauce over the meatballs
and serve immediately.

The Chicken Puffs are eaten with the fingers, as a starter. The Golden Dumplings are fiddly to prepare until you have had some practice, but on the other hand the prawns are quick and easy to do. Menu serves 5-6.

Dry-Fried Chicken in Lettuce Puffs

生菜包鸡

3 skinned chicken breasts, about
    225 g (8 oz)
100 g (4 oz) chicken livers, cleaned,
    washed and dried
600 ml (1 pint) vegetable oil, plus
    1 tablespoon
2.5 cm (1 inch) piece root ginger,
    peeled and finely chopped
2 spring onions, finely chopped
½ cucumber, finely diced
5 cm (2 inch) piece canned bamboo
    shoot, finely diced
25 g (1 oz) frozen peas, thawed
50 g (2 oz) dried Chinese
    mushrooms, soaked for
    20 minutes, drained, stemmed
    and sliced

100 g (4 oz) canned water
    chestnuts, drained and finely
    diced
pinch of salt
pinch of sugar
1 teaspoon dark soy sauce
pinch of MSG
pinch of freshly ground white pepper
1 tablespoon Chinese wine or dry
    sherry
100 ml (3½ fl oz) chicken stock
25 g (1 oz) cornflour
½ teaspoon sesame oil
50 g (2 oz) rice noodles
1 lettuce, leaves separated, washed
    and dried

Preparation time: 40 minutes,
    plus soaking
Cooking time: about 5-10
    minutes

1. Chop the chicken breasts and chicken livers together finely.
2. Heat 1 tablespoon oil in a wok, then add the ginger and spring onions. Stir-fry for 30 seconds then add the chicken and stir-fry until dry.

Left to right: Dry-Fried Chicken in Lettuce Puffs, Golden Egg Dumplings with Chinese Mushrooms, Quick Fry Prawns

Golden Egg Dumplings with Chinese Mushrooms

香
菇
蛋
餃

100 g (4 oz) minced pork
50 g (2 oz) peeled prawns, minced
1 tablespoon mustard greens,
    chopped
1 spring onion, finely chopped
1 teaspoon salt
pinch of freshly ground white pepper
1 tablespoon Chinese wine or dry
    sherry
1½ teaspoons sugar
1 teaspoon sesame oil
2 pinches of MSG
5 tablespoons water
4 eggs, beaten
250 ml (8 fl oz) chicken stock
6 dried Chinese mushrooms, soaked
    for 20 minutes, drained, stemmed
    and sliced
1 tablespoon vegetable oil
5 cm (2 inch) piece canned bamboo
    shoot, thinly sliced
50 g (2 oz) mangetout
1 tablespoon soy sauce
1 teaspoon sesame oil
1 teaspoon cornflour

**Preparation time: 10 minutes,
    plus soaking**
**Cooking time: approximately
    1 hour**

---

1. Mix together the minced pork and minced prawns. Add the chopped mustard greens, finely chopped spring onion, salt, white pepper, wine, 1 teaspoon sugar, sesame oil, 1 pinch MSG, and 4 tablespoons water, and mix well together.
2. Heat a well-oiled crêpe pan until the oil starts to smoke, then add 1 tablespoon beaten egg to form a thin round pancake about 6 cm (2½ inches) in diameter. Place a heaped teaspoon of the meat just below the centre of the pancake and then fold over the pancake to form a little parcel. Cook over low heat until the dumpling is lightly browned on both sides. Repeat until all the egg is used.
3. Place all the egg dumplings in a pan and add the chicken stock and Chinese mushrooms. Bring to the boil and simmer for about 20 minutes. Remove the dumplings and mushrooms from the stock, drain and reserve in a bowl.
4. Heat a wok over high heat for 30 seconds and add 1 tablespoon oil. Drop in the sliced bamboo shoots, mangetout and reserved mushrooms. Stir-fry together, then add the soy sauce, sesame oil, remaining sugar and MSG, plus the remaining stock.
5. Arrange the dumplings on a serving dish. Blend the cornflour and 1 tablespoon water, and stir into the wok to thicken the sauce. Pour the sauce over the dumplings and serve.

3. Add the cucumber, bamboo shoot, frozen peas, Chinese mushrooms and water chestnuts. Stir-fry together.
4. Add the salt, sugar, dark soy sauce, MSG, white pepper and wine and mix together thoroughly.
5. Blend the chicken stock with the cornflour and stir into the wok to form a sauce. There should only be a small amount of sauce, just enough to moisten the meat and vegetables.
6. Heat the 600 ml (1 pint) vegetable oil in another wok and when it reaches 180°C/350°F, or when a cube of bread browns in 30 seconds, carefully put in the rice noodles. They should immediately puff up. Lift them out of the oil and drain on paper towels. Arrange on a serving dish and pour the chicken mixture on top.
7. To serve, put a little of the chicken, vegetables and rice noodles onto a lettuce leaf, roll up and eat, using your fingers.

Quick Fry Prawns

炒
蝦
仁

450 g (1 lb) uncooked prawns,
    peeled and deveined
1 egg white
1 tablespoon cornflour
600 ml (1 pint) vegetable oil
2.5 cm (1 inch) piece root ginger,
    peeled and finely chopped
1 small onion, finely chopped
1 teaspoon salt
pinch of MSG
2 tablespoons chicken stock
1 tablespoon Chinese wine or dry
    sherry
1 teaspoon wine vinegar

Preparation time: 5 minutes
Cooking time: 4-5 minutes

---

1. Put the prawns, egg white and cornflour in a bowl and mix well together. Heat the oil in a wok, then add the coated prawns. Stir-fry the prawns for about 1½ minutes, then remove from the oil and drain on paper towels.
2. Pour off most of the oil, leaving enough just to coat the bottom of the wok. Reheat the wok and add the ginger, onion, salt, MSG, stock and wine. Bring to the boil and simmer until the sauce has reduced by half.
3. Return the prawns to the wok and toss together with the other ingredients for about 30 seconds. Finally, sprinkle on the vinegar. Serve immediately.

An attractive, light meal which could be served with rice. The unusual kidney dish is made by scoring the kidneys deeply with criss-cross cuts. When placed in hot water, they curl up to resemble flowers. Menu serves 4.

Spiced Kidneys

450 g (1 lb) pigs' kidneys, cut in half
   lengthways, skinned and cored
600 ml (1 pint) vegetable oil
5 cm (2 inch) piece root ginger,
   peeled and finely chopped
1 garlic clove, crushed
4 spring onions, cut into 2.5 cm
   (1 inch) pieces
5 cm (2 inch) piece canned bamboo
   shoot, cut into shreds
100 ml (3½ fl oz) chicken stock
2 teaspoons soy sauce
1 tablespoon Chinese wine or dry
   sherry
pinch of 5-spice powder
pinch of sugar
pinch of MSG
2 teaspoons cornflour
1 tablespoon water

Preparation time: 20 minutes
Cooking time: 10 minutes

1. Lay each half kidney flat side down on a board. With a sharp knife, make cuts about 5 mm (¼ inch) apart lengthways down the kidney. Don't go right through. Now cut the kidney in a similar fashion crosswise except making each alternate cut sever the kidney into slices. You should now have 1 cm (½ inch) wide slices of kidney with a deep cut running down the middle.
2. Fill a pan with water, bring to the boil and put in the kidney slices. They should all curl up to form flowers. When the water comes to the boil again, lift out the kidneys immediately and drain. Refresh under cold water and dry on paper towels.
3. Heat the oil in a wok, add the ginger and garlic and then put in the kidney flowers. Stir-fry very quickly for about 2 minutes, then lift out and drain on paper towels. Keep warm.

4. Pour off most of the oil, leaving about 1 tablespoon of oil to coat the bottom of the wok. Reheat the wok, then put in the spring onions, bamboo shoots, and kidneys all together. Add the chicken stock, soy sauce, wine, 5-spice powder, sugar and MSG. Blend the cornflour with 1 tablespoon of cold water and stir in to thicken the sauce.
5. Pour into a serving dish and serve immediately.

Below: Spiced Kidneys
Right: Stir-Fried Beansprouts with Vinegar Sauce, Steamed Egg with Crab Meat

Stir-Fried Beansprouts with Vinegar Sauce

3 tablespoons vegetable oil
450 g (1 lb) beansprouts
1 green pepper, cored, seeded and cut into shreds
1 teaspoon salt
pinch of MSG
1 tablespoon wine vinegar
1 teaspoon cornflour
1 tablespoon water

Preparation time: 5 minutes
Cooking time: 5 minutes

1. Heat the oil in a wok. Add the beansprouts and green pepper and stir-fry together for 1 minute. Sprinkle on the salt, MSG and vinegar.
2. Blend the cornflour with the water and stir into the mixture until the sauce has thickened. Turn out onto a serving dish and serve at once. The beansprouts and green pepper should still be a little crunchy.

Steamed Egg with Crab Meat

150 ml (¼ pint) water
pinch of MSG
½ teaspoon salt
2 egg yolks and 3 egg whites, beaten together
1 tablespoon Chinese wine or dry sherry
pinch of cornflour
100 g (4 oz) crab meat, flaked, with a few pieces left whole to decorate
chopped parsley, to garnish

Preparation time: 10 minutes
Cooking time: 15 minutes

1. Add the water, MSG and salt to the beaten eggs and mix well.
2. Add the Chinese wine and cornflour to the crab meat and stir into the egg mixture. Pour the egg and crab mixture into a large heatproof dish and place in a steamer for 10 minutes.
3. Gently place the reserved pieces of crab on top of the egg and steam for another 5 minutes. Sprinkle the chopped parsley on top and serve hot.

An elegant and impressive menu, ideal for a special occasion. Serves 6.

Crispy Chicken Rolls Stuffed with Asparagus

2 chicken breasts, skinned, and cut into thin slices, beaten flat
pinch of salt
pinch of freshly ground white pepper
pinch of MSG
½ teaspoon sesame oil
8-10 canned asparagus spears
2 spring onions, finely shredded
2 slices root ginger, peeled and shredded
plain flour, for dusting
100 g (4 oz) self-raising flour
1 egg, lightly beaten
2 tablespoons water
1 litre (1¾ pints) vegetable oil

Preparation time: 20 minutes, plus marinating
Cooking time: 3-5 minutes

1. Carefully toss the chicken slices in the salt, pepper, MSG, and sesame oil. Leave to marinate for about 1 hour.
2. Place one asparagus spear, and a little spring onion and shredded ginger, on each slice of chicken and form into a roll. Make sure the filling is completely enclosed in the chicken meat, then dust lightly with flour.
3. Beat the self-raising flour, egg and water together to make a batter. If the batter seems too thick, thin it down with a little more water.
4. Heat the vegetable oil in a wok to 180°C/350°F, or until a cube of bread browns in 30 seconds. Dip the rolls into the batter, then lower them into the hot oil. Deep-fry gently for about 3 minutes or until the rolls are golden brown all over. Remove from the oil and drain thoroughly on paper towels.

Fish in Tomato Sauce

450 g (1 lb) sole or plaice fillets, cut into strips 2.5 cm (1 inch) long and 2 cm (¾ inch) wide
1 egg white
1 tablespoon cornflour
pinch of salt
1 tablespoon Chinese wine or dry sherry
pinch of freshly ground white pepper
1.2 litres (2 pints) vegetable oil
Sauce:
1 onion, peeled and diced
3 canned pineapple rings, diced
1 green pepper, cored, seeded and diced
3 tablespoons sugar
3 tablespoons vinegar
6 tablespoons water
3 tablespoons tomato purée
1 tablespoon Chinese wine or dry sherry
2 teaspoons cornflour
pinch of salt
1 teaspoon sesame oil
To garnish:
1 tomato, sliced
1 lemon, quartered

Preparation time: 20-30 minutes
Cooking time: about 15 minutes

1. Marinate the fish strips in the egg white, cornflour, salt, wine and white pepper for 20-30 minutes.
2. Heat the oil in a wok to 180°C/350°F or until a cube of bread browns in 30 seconds. Fry the fish gently until golden brown, then lift out and drain on paper towels.
3. Pour off most of the cooking oil, leaving just enough to coat the bottom, and reheat the wok. Add the onion, pineapple, and green pepper to the wok and stir-fry together for about 30 seconds. Mix together the sugar, vinegar, water, tomato purée, wine, cornflour, salt and sesame oil, and add to the vegetables.
4. Bring to the boil, stirring. If the sauce becomes too thick add a little more water. Pour this sauce over the fish or use it as a dip. Garnish with the tomato slices and lemon quarters.

Chrysanthemum Pork Balls

菊
花
肉
丸

225 g (8 oz) minced pork
75 g (3 oz) dried shrimps, soaked for 20 minutes, drained, then minced
25 g (1 oz) dried Chinese mushrooms, soaked for 20 minutes, drained, stemmed and sliced
2 spring onions, finely chopped
2.5 cm (1 inch) piece root ginger, peeled and finely chopped
75 g (3 oz) cornflour
½ teaspoon salt
pinch of MSG
pinch of freshly ground white pepper
1 egg white
5 whole eggs
600 ml (1 pint) vegetable oil, plus 3-4 tablespoons

Preparation time: 15 minutes, plus soaking
Cooking time: about 10 minutes

1. In a bowl mix together the pork, shrimps and Chinese mushrooms. Add the finely chopped spring onions and ginger, and then the cornflour, salt, MSG, white pepper and egg white. Mix together thoroughly, to ensure that the cornflour and egg white bind the mixture together.
2. Beat the 5 whole eggs together. Heat a wok, add 1 tablespoon oil and pour in a quarter of the egg to make a large, thin omelette. Turn carefully to cook on both sides, then lift out on to a plate. Repeat until the egg is used up, adding more oil as required and reheating the wok each time. Shred the omelettes finely and set aside.
3. Using about 2 teaspoons of the minced pork mixture at a time, roll into balls. Coat with the shredded egg. Continue until all the minced pork is used up.
4. Heat the vegetable oil in a wok, then put in the coated pork balls. Fry gently for about 3 minutes until cooked through and golden brown on the outside. Serve on a lettuce leaf surrounded by orange and lemon slices.

Clockwise from the bottom: Fish in Tomato Sauce, Crispy Chicken Rolls Stuffed with Asparagus, Chrysanthemum Pork Balls

Nanking is famous for its ducks. Every village in this region has its own pond or stream, where ducks are reared in great numbers. Serve this meal with beansprout salad and rice. Serves 6-8.

Shanghai Baked Sea Bass

1 *sea bass or plaice, about 750 g (1½ lb)*
1 *teaspoon salt*
1 *teaspoon freshly ground black pepper*
1 *teaspoon ground ginger*
1 *teaspoon salted black beans, soaked, drained and crushed*
1 *tablespoon soy sauce*
1 *teaspoon sugar*
1 *tablespoon Chinese wine or dry sherry*
1 *tablespoon shredded root ginger*
2 *spring onions, cut into 5 cm (2 inch) lengths*
2 *tablespoons peanut oil*
To finish:
1 *tablespoon soy sauce*
1 *teaspoon sesame oil*

Preparation time: 15 minutes
Cooking time: 20 minutes
Oven: 180°C, 350°F, Gas Mark 4

1. Wash the fish and dry on paper towels. Using a sharp knife, make deep criss-cross cuts down each side of the fish. Mix the salt, pepper and ground ginger together and rub into the cuts and on the inside of the fish.
2. In a bowl, mix together the crushed black beans, soy sauce, sugar, and Chinese wine. Arrange the shredded ginger and spring onions on the bottom of an ovenproof dish. Lay the fish on top.
3. Heat the peanut oil in a small pan until smoking. Pour this over the fish and then spread on the black bean mixture. Cover the fish tightly with foil and put into a preheated oven for about 15 minutes, or until the fish is firm to the touch. When ready to serve, mix 1 tablespoon soy sauce and 1 teaspoon sesame oil together and spoon this over the fish. Serve immediately.

Nanking Salt Water Duck

2 *teaspoons Szechuan peppercorns*
3 *tablespoons salt*
1 *duck, about 2 kg (5 lb)*
Sauce:
1 × 225 g (8 oz) *can yellow bean paste*
2 *tablespoons sugar*
2 *tablespoons vegetable oil*
2 *tablespoons water*

Preparation time: 15 minutes, plus marinating
Cooking time: 1 hour

1. Heat a wok, add the peppercorns and salt and dry fry for 1 minute, then remove.
2. Rub the duck inside and out with the peppercorn-salt mixture, then place in a tightly covered pan. Leave to season for 24 hours, turning once or twice during this time.
3. Remove the duck from the pan, wash well and dry on paper towels. Place the duck in a large bowl and steam over high heat for 50 minutes. At the end of this time turn off the heat, but leave the duck in the steamer until it is cold.
4. Remove the duck when cold and chop into rectangular pieces, including the bones. Mix all the sauce ingredients in a small pan and simmer for 5 minutes, stirring. Arrange the duck on a serving plate and pour on the sauce. Serve cold.

Left: Shanghai Baked Sea Bass
Right: Nanking Salt Water Duck

Serve this meal with rice or noodles. The delicious Crispy Spring Rolls, which are smaller and thinner than ordinary ones, can be served on their own, as a snack or as a starter. Menu serves 4.

Spring Onions Smothered Trout

1 trout, about 500 g (1½ lb)
2 teaspoons salt
2 tablespoons soy sauce
2 teaspoons sesame oil, plus extra for drizzling
1-2 tablespoons sugar
1½ tablespoons vinegar
½ teaspoon freshly ground white pepper
2 tablespoons vegetable oil
1 garlic clove, crushed
225 g (8 oz) spring onions, cut into 1 cm (½ inch) lengths

1 cm (½ inch) piece root ginger, peeled and shredded
250 ml (8 fl oz) water

Preparation time: 15 minutes
Cooking time: about 1¼ hours

1. Rub the trout with the salt, then rinse and dry on paper towels.
2. In a bowl, mix together the soy sauce, sesame oil, sugar, vinegar, and white pepper, and reserve. Heat the oil in a wok. Add the garlic to flavour the oil, then put in the fish and shallow fry on both sides for about 2 minutes. Lift out the fish and drain on paper towels. Discard the garlic.
3. Pour off the oil, leaving just enough to coat the bottom of the wok. Put a layer of spring onions and ginger in the bottom of the wok, then lay the fish on top. Place the remaining spring onions and ginger on top of the fish and pour on the sauce. Add the water and bring to the boil. Lower the heat and simmer for at least 1 hour.
4. Test if the fish is cooked by inserting a chopstick. If it goes in easily, the fish is cooked. Lift the fish and spring onions carefully out of the wok onto a warmed serving dish and drizzle on a few extra drops of sesame oil.

Crispy Spring Rolls, Shanghai Style

上海式春捲

225 g (8 oz) lean pork, shredded
1 tablespoon soy sauce
1 tablespoon Chinese wine or dry
    sherry
1 teaspoon cornflour, plus extra for
    dusting
600 ml (1 pint) vegetable oil, plus
    2 tablespoons
50 g (2 oz) mustard greens, chopped
6 dried Chinese mushrooms, soaked
    for 20 minutes, stemmed and
    finely shredded
1 small leek, finely shredded
5 cm (2½ inch) piece canned
    bamboo shoot, finely shredded
½ teaspoon salt
pinch of freshly ground white pepper
pinch of sugar
1 packet frozen ready-made spring
    roll wrappers, thawed
600 ml (1 pint) vegetable oil

Vinegar dip:
1 tablespoon finely shredded root
    ginger
2 tablespoons wine vinegar

Preparation time: 30 minutes,
plus soaking and marinating
Cooking time: 15 minutes

1. Marinate the shredded pork in the soy sauce, Chinese wine and cornflour for 15 minutes.
2. Heat 2 tablespoons of the oil in a wok. When hot, add the mustard, greens and pork and stir-fry together until the pork changes colour. Transfer to a bowl and reheat the wok. Add the Chinese mushrooms and stir-fry with the leek, bamboo shoot, salt, white pepper, and sugar. Return the cooked pork and mustard greens to the wok and mix all together. Pour the mixture into a bowl and leave to cool.
3. To assemble the spring rolls, cut the ready-made spring roll wrappers in half on the diagonal. Place 1 tablespoon of filling about 1 cm (½ inch) from the long diagonal side and then fold in the sides and roll up neatly, enclosing all the filling. Seal the pastry with a little water and lay on a tray dusted with cornflour. The rolls can be frozen like this or kept in the refrigerator until ready for use.
4. To cook the spring rolls, heat the 600 ml (1 pint) oil in a wok or deep frier to 180°C/350°F, or until a cube of bread browns in 30 seconds. Lower the spring rolls into the hot oil and deep-fry gently until golden brown and crisp. Drain on paper towels. Serve hot, with the ginger and vinegar mixed to make the dip.

Deep-Fried Pork Strips

油炸肉條

450 g (1 lb) belly of pork
1 tablespoon Chinese wine or dry
    sherry
pinch of ginger
1 teaspoon salt
1 teaspoon sesame oil
pinch of freshly ground white pepper
1 egg
50 g (2 oz) plain flour
1 coriander sprig, chopped
600 ml (1 pint) vegetable oil, plus
    1 tablespoon
Dip:
1 spring onion, finely chopped
1 teaspoon chopped root ginger
1 garlic clove, crushed
1½ tablespoons wine vinegar
1 tablespoon tomato ketchup
4 tablespoons water, plus 1 teaspoon
pinch of salt
½ teaspoon cornflour
coriander sprigs, to garnish

Preparation time: 10 minutes,
plus marinating
Cooking time: 15 minutes

1. Slice the pork into 1 cm (½ inch) slices and then cut into strips. Add the wine, ginger, salt, sesame oil and white pepper, and mix well together. Leave to marinate for 30 minutes.
2. In a separate bowl, mix together the egg, plain flour and chopped coriander.
3. Heat 1 tablespoon oil in a wok. Add the spring onion, root ginger and crushed garlic. Fry gently until fragrant. Blend the cornflour with 1 teaspoon water, then add the vinegar, tomato ketchup, water, salt and cornflour to the wok. Let the liquid come to the boil, then pour it into a small bowl. Set aside to use as a dip.
4. Heat the remaining oil to 180°C/350°F or until a cube of bread browns in 30 seconds. Toss the pork strips in the egg and flour mixture until well coated. Lower the strips into the oil and fry gently until golden brown. Lift the pork strips from the oil with a perforated spoon and drain on paper towels.
5. Reheat the oil again and deep-fry the pork strips again for 1 minute. Remove from the oil and drain on paper towels. Place on a warm serving dish and garnish with coriander sprigs. Use the sauce as a dip.

Left to right: Spring Onions Smothered Trout, Crispy Spring Rolls, Shanghai Style, with Vinegar Dip, Deep-Fried Pork Strips with Dip

These desserts could be served with any of the suggested menus. Eight Treasure Rice is a sweet steamed pudding, made of glutinous rice, which resembles a colourful Christmas pudding. It is served in China on special occasions, such as the New Year.

Sticky Rice Cakes with Red Bean Paste

225 g (8 oz) flaked rice
100 g (4 oz) plain flour
5 tablespoons red bean paste
150 ml (¼ pint) vegetable oil
2 tablespoons sugar

Preparation time: 5 minutes
Cooking time: 35-40 minutes

1. Place the flaked rice in a bowl with enough water to cover, place in a steamer and steam for about 30 minutes.
2. Remove the rice from the steamer, turn out and mix with the plain flour. Knead together to form a dough. Divide into about 14 even-sized pieces. Roll these into balls and then flatten them with the palm of your hand. Put about 2-3 teaspoons of red bean paste in the centre of the dough and then bring up the sides to completely enclose the red bean paste. Flatten again to about 2.5 cm (1 inch) thick.
3. Heat the oil in a wok to 180°C/350°F or until a cube of bread browns in 30 seconds and then put the rice cakes into the oil. Fry gently for 3 minutes on each side or until golden brown, then lift out and drain on paper towels. Sprinkle with sugar and serve immediately.

Hsing-Ren-Tou-Fu (Almond Float)

300 ml (½ pint) cold water
2 packets unflavoured gelatin
300 ml (½ pint) milk
1 tablespoon almond extract
1 × 185 g (6½ oz) can mandarin
    orange segments
Syrup:
100 g (4 oz) sugar
500 ml (18 fl oz) cold water

**Preparation time: 5 minutes,
    plus setting
Cooking time: 15 minutes**

1. In a large bowl, mix together 100 ml (3½ fl oz) of the cold water and the gelatin and let it soften for about 5 minutes. Bring the remaining water to the boil in a small pan and then add the gelatin mixture. Stir over heat until it becomes clear, then stir in the milk and almond extract. Pour it all into a shallow dish and leave it to set in a cool place.
2. Make the syrup while the jelly is setting by combining the sugar and water in a small pan and bringing it to the boil. Stir and mix well. Cool in the refrigerator. This sauce will be thin.
3. When set, cut the almond jelly into squares or diamond shapes and arrange on a dish. Decorate with the mandarin segments and serve with the syrup.

Above: Sticky Rice Cakes with Red Bean Paste, Hsing-Ren-Tou-Fu (Almond Float) Right: Eight Treasure Rice

Eight Treasure Rice

200 g (7 oz) dates, stoned and
    chopped
1 × 225 g (8 oz) can red bean paste
450 g (1 lb) glutinous rice
600 ml (1 pint) cold water
40 g (1½ oz) lard, melted
2 tablespoons sugar
25 g (1 oz) angelica
red and green glacé cherries
2 oz flaked almonds
Syrup:
100 g (4 oz) sugar
250 ml (8 fl oz) cold water
1 teaspoon almond essence
1 tablespoon cornflour
3 tablespoons water

Preparation time: 15 minutes
Cooking time: 1 hour

1. Mix the chopped dates with the red bean paste.
2. Rinse the rice, drain, then place in a 2 litre (3½ pint) saucepan and add the cold water. Bring to the boil, then simmer for about 25 minutes. Stir in 2 tablespoons of lard and 2 tablespoons of sugar. Mix well.
3. Grease a 1.2 litre (2 pint) heatproof bowl and line it with three-quarters of the cooked rice. Spoon the bean paste mixture on to the rice and then place the remaining rice on top. Spread the rice evenly and press down flat with the palm of your hand. Put a plate over the bowl and unmould the pudding carefully onto a serving dish.
4. Decorate the top of the pudding with the angelica, red and green glacé cherries and flaked almonds in an attractive pattern. Cover the pudding with cling film then put the original bowl back over the pudding and turn it back into the bowl. Remove the plate and cover the top with cling film. Steam the pudding for at least 1 hour. This pudding can be reheated.
5. While the pudding is steaming make up the syrup. Combine the sugar and water in a small pan and boil until the sugar dissolves. Add the almond essence. Blend the cornflour and water and stir in to thicken the sauce.
6. When ready to serve, unmould the pudding carefully and peel off the cling film. Pour the hot syrup over the top and serve at once.

南部∴廣東

Patrick Procktor

The southern province of Canton, with its mild, semi-tropical climate, grows an abundance of produce all year round: rice, fruit and vegetables enjoy four seasons, while plentiful feed for livestock means that high-quality meat and poultry is abundant. And the long coastline gives access to the rich fishing grounds of the South China Sea with their enormous variety of fish and seafood. No wonder that for centuries the Cantonese have been noted for their sophisticated cuisine, and their keen interest in food. In Canton, people greet each by saying 'Have you eaten?' – literally 'Have you had rice?' – as we would say 'Good morning' or 'How are you?'

Of all the regional styles, Cantonese is the best known in the west, largely because the first Chinese to emigrate in large numbers in the 19th century came from this region. Because their food is of such superlative quality, the Cantonese are connoisseurs of flavour and taste. They prefer cooking methods such as steaming or ·poaching, which preserve the natural flavours and colours. Steamed scallops with black bean sauce, for example, is a delicious speciality. The Cantonese have also developed a cooking method called Cha Siu which can be translated as 'barbecue roasting'. This involves marinating meat, especially pork, for some time and then roasting it quickly in a very hot oven.

As so much of the province lies on the coast, seafood plays an important part in the cuisine of Southern China. Prawns, shrimps, scallops, lobster and crab are in plentiful supply – they are stir-fried or steamed, usually with ginger and onion to offset their 'fishiness'. Seafood flavours are also frequently used in meat dishes – giving the food a distinctive savoury quality. Oyster sauce, shrimp sauce and shrimp paste are widely used – beef with oyster sauce is a favourite dish.

In this lush climate fresh vegetables are in abundance and are used extensively. Cantonese cooking specialises in the quick stir-frying of vegetables, which helps to retain colour, flavour and nutrients. Spinach, cabbage, peppers, broccoli and dried mushrooms are widely used. Fruit is also abundant, and so it is perhaps natural that fruit is often combined in dishes with meat or poultry.

Cantonese food is noted for its frequent use of seafood, and seafood-flavoured sauces. It is also noted for its fruit — oranges, tangerines, plums, loquats, bananas, lychees, etc. Fruit flavours and fruit juices are often used in savoury dishes, particularly in sweet and sour dishes as here. Menu serves 4.

Cantonese Fried Rice

4 tablespoons vegetable oil
3 eggs, beaten
50 g (2 oz) cha shao (ready-cooked
    pork), diced
50 g (2 oz) peeled prawns
100 g (4 oz) green peas, lightly
    cooked
1 teaspoon salt
2 spring onions, finely chopped
450 g (1 lb) cooked rice
1½ tablespoons soy sauce

Preparation time: 15 minutes
Cooking time: 8 minutes

1. Heat a wok over high heat, then add 1½ tablespoons oil. When the oil is hot, add the beaten eggs. Stir-fry until scrambled, then remove to a plate and break up into small pieces with a fork.
2. Heat another 1½ tablespoons of the oil in the wok and add the diced cha shao, together with the prawns, green peas and salt. Stir-fry for 1 minute, then remove from the wok.
3. Heat the remaining oil in the wok then add the spring onions and cooked rice. Stir to heat the rice through and separate the grains, then add the eggs, cha shao, prawns, peas and soy sauce. Toss together so that everything is well mixed, and serve.

Sweet and Sour Fish

450 g (1 lb) white fish fillets, cut into
    4 cm (1½ inch) slices
5 tablespoons cornflour, plus
    1 teaspoon
1 egg
1 tablespoon cold water
600 ml (1 pint) vegetable oil
2 slices root ginger, finely chopped
2 spring onions, finely chopped
50 g (2 oz) frozen peas
1 carrot, peeled and cut into rings
50 g (2 oz) canned bamboo shoots,
    drained and diced
2 tablespoons tomato ketchup
2 tablespoons wine vinegar
2 tablespoons orange juice
2 tablespoons sugar
1 teaspoon salt
2 tablespoons chicken stock

Preparation time: 15 minutes,
    plus soaking
Cooking time: 15 minutes

1. Dust the fish strips with a little cornflour. Mix 4 tablespoons cornflour with the egg and cold water to form a batter.

2. Heat the oil in a wok to 180°C/350°F or until a cube of bread browns in 30 seconds. Dip the fish in the batter and deep-fry piece by piece for about 2 minutes, or until golden brown. Remove and drain on paper towels.
3. Pour off all but 1 tablespoon of oil from the wok. Add the ginger, spring onions, peas, carrot and bamboo shoots.
4. In a bowl mix together the tomato ketchup, vinegar, orange juice, sugar and salt. Add the mixture to the wok and stir all together.
5. Blend 1 teaspoon of cornflour with the chicken stock and add to the wok. Bring to the boil and stir until the sauce thickens and becomes translucent. Add the fish pieces, turn in the sauce for 30 seconds, then serve on a heated serving dish.

Left to right: Cantonese Fried Rice, Sweet and Sour Fish, Chinese Mushroom Soup
Illustration: Gardens at Yuan Ming Yuan.

Chinese Mushroom Soup

600 ml (1 pint) chicken stock
6 dried Chinese mushrooms, soaked
   for 20 minutes, drained, stemmed
   and thinly sliced
2 tablespoons cornflour
2 tablespoons water
3 egg whites
1 spring onion, finely chopped

Preparation time: 20 minutes,
  plus soaking
Cooking time: 7 minutes

1. Bring the chicken stock to the boil in a pan then add the sliced mushrooms. Simmer for 3 minutes.
2. Blend together the cornflour and water and stir into the soup until it thickens.
3. Lightly beat the egg whites and pour into the soup in a slow steady stream, stirring all the time. Bring back to the boil then pour into a tureen. Serve with a sprinkling of spring onion on top.

A typical Cantonese meal which has a strong seafood flavour. Fish balls can be bought ready-made in Chinese supermarkets, or you can make your own (see below). Chow Mein, served with a meaty sauce, makes a good filling accompaniment to any meal. Menu serves 4.

To make fish balls, finely mince 100 g (4 oz) fillet of white fish such as cod or plaice. Beat well in a bowl with 1 egg, 1 tablespoon cornflour and a few drops of oil. Place in the refrigerator for 1 hour, then roll into walnut-sized balls and keep chilled.

Three Seafoods Stir-Fry

炒
三
鮮

100 g (4 oz) uncooked prawns, peeled and deveined
100 g (4 oz) scallops, sliced in half
100 g (4 oz) squid, cleaned and sliced
25 g (1 oz) cornflour
1 egg white
600 ml (1 pint) vegetable oil
2 sticks of celery, sliced into 2.5 cm (1 inch) pieces
1 carrot, scraped and cut into rings
2 spring onions, finely chopped
2.5 cm (1 inch) piece root ginger, peeled and finely chopped
2 garlic cloves, crushed
100 ml (3½ fl oz) chicken stock
large pinch of MSG
½ teaspoon salt
1 tablespoon Chinese wine or dry sherry
few drops sesame oil
1 teaspoon vinegar

Preparation time: 30 minutes
Cooking time: about 5 minutes

1. Mix the prepared seafood with three-quarters of the cornflour and egg white, mixed together.
2. Heat the oil to 180°C/350°F or until a cube of bread browns in 30 seconds. Add the seafood, celery and carrot. Stir-fry together for about 2 minutes, then remove from the oil and drain on paper towels.
3. Pour off most of the oil, leaving enough to coat the bottom of the wok. Reheat the wok, then put in the spring onions, ginger, garlic, chicken stock, MSG, salt and wine. Bring to the boil, then mix in the remaining cornflour and egg white to thicken the sauce. Return the seafood and vegetables to the wok. Drizzle on the sesame oil and vinegar, toss together and serve immediately.

Left to right: Three Seafoods Stir-Fry, Chow Mein (Fried Noodles), Fish Balls with Vegetable Soup

Chow Mein (Fried Noodles)

450 g (1 lb) egg noodles
275 g (10 oz) pork fillet, shredded
2 teaspoons cornflour
5 tablespoons vegetable oil
100 g (4 oz) canned bamboo shoots, drained and shredded
½ cucumber, shredded
100 g (4 oz) spinach leaves, shredded

Sauce:
3 tablespoons soy sauce
2 tablespoons Chinese wine or dry sherry
1 teaspoon salt
1 teaspoon sugar
1 teaspoon cornflour
1 teaspoon sesame oil

Preparation time: 20 minutes
Cooking time: about 12 minutes

1. Plunge the noodles into a pan of boiling water and simmer for 10 minutes or until soft but not sticky. Drain and refresh in cold running water.
2. Toss the shredded pork with the cornflour.
3. Heat about half the oil in a wok or frying pan. Place the noodles in a large bowl, tossing with a fork to separate them, then pour over the hot oil. Stir to ensure that the noodles are evenly coated. Return the noodles to the wok and stir-fry for 2-3 minutes. Remove the noodles with a slotted spoon and place on a serving dish.
4. Heat the remaining oil in the wok and quickly stir-fry the pork, bamboo shoots, cucumber and spinach for 3 minutes. Mix together the sauce ingredients and pour into the wok. Cook for about 2 minutes, then pour the mixture over the noodles, sprinkle with sesame oil and serve.

Fish Balls with Vegetable Soup

600 ml (1 pint) chicken stock or water
100 g (4 oz) ready-made fish balls
50 g (2 oz) mushrooms, thinly sliced
50 g (2 oz) cooked ham, thinly sliced
50 g (2 oz) canned bamboo shoots, drained and thinly sliced
salt
chopped coriander, to garnish

Preparation time: 5 minutes
Cooking time: 5 minutes

1. Bring the stock to a rolling boil, add the fish balls, and as soon as they float to the surface, add the mushrooms, ham and bamboo shoots, then boil together for 1 minute.
2. Sprinkle with coriander just before serving.

A well-balanced meal for 4. The highly savoury taste of the beef comes from the use of salted black beans, which are first soaked and drained, then mashed into the cooking oil over a high heat. Begin with the delicate, creamy soup — a favourite soup of the region and one which is often served at banquets.

Velvet Chicken and Sweetcorn Soup

1.2 litres (2 pints) chicken stock
1 × 225 g (8 oz) can creamed
   sweetcorn
½ teaspoon salt
pinch of MSG
2 tablespoons cornflour
4 tablespoons cold water
2 spring onions, finely chopped
2 egg whites
2 tablespoons milk
50 g (2 oz) chopped ham

Preparation time: 10 minutes
Cooking time: 10 minutes

1. Put the stock in a pan and bring to the boil. Add the creamed corn, salt, MSG, and the cornflour blended with the water. Stir until the soup thickens and comes back to the boil. Sprinkle on the spring onions, then turn off the heat.
2. Beat together the egg whites and milk and pour on to the soup in a thin stream.
3. Pour into individual bowls and sprinkle on the chopped ham. Serve immediately.

Quick-Fried Beef in Black Bean Sauce

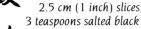

2½ tablespoons vegetable oil
450 g (1 lb) beef steak, cut into
   2.5 cm (1 inch) slices
3 teaspoons salted black beans,
   soaked in 3 tablespoons water for
   20 minutes
½ teaspoon chilli sauce
2 red or green peppers, cored, seeded
   and cut into 2.5 cm (1 inch)
   squares
1 tablespoon cornflour
3 tablespoons water or beef stock
1 tablespoon Chinese wine or sherry

Preparation time: 15 minutes,
   plus soaking
Cooking time: 6 minutes

1. Heat the oil in a wok until smoking and add the beef. Stir-fry quickly for about 1 minute, then remove and drain on paper towels.
2. Add the black beans and the soaking water to the wok. Mash the beans in the wok then add the chilli sauce and peppers. Stir all together and return the beef to the wok.
3. Blend the cornflour with the stock and stir into the wok to thicken the sauce. Add the wine and stir to mix until the sauce has thickened.

Prawn Noodles

100 g (4 oz) uncooked prawns,
   peeled and deveined
1 egg white
1 teaspoon cornflour
350 g (12 oz) egg noodles
3 tablespoons vegetable oil
3 spring onions, cut into 2.5 cm
   (1 inch) lengths
Sauce:
2 tablespoons soy sauce
1 tablespoon Chinese wine or dry
   sherry
1 teaspoon sugar
1 teaspoon sesame oil

Preparation time: 12 minutes
Cooking time: 5 minutes

1. Mix the prawns with the egg white and cornflour.
2. Put the noodles in boiling water, boil for about 5 minutes, then drain and rinse under cold running water.
3. Heat the oil in a wok, add the spring onions with the prawns, soy sauce, wine and sugar and stir-fry for 1 minute. Add the noodles to the wok and mix well. Cook for 2-3 minutes, then add the sesame oil.

Clockwise from the back: Velvet Chicken and Sweetcorn Soup, Prawn Noodles, Quick-Fried Beef in Black Bean Sauce

Fruit abounds in this region and is often used in savoury dishes. Almost any kind of fruit juice can be added to the sweet and sour pork to give added flavour — orange juice or pineapple juice are particular favourites. Menu serves 4, with rice as an accompaniment.

Chinese Cabbage and Mushrooms

3 tablespoons vegetable oil
450 g (1 lb) Chinese cabbage, cut
    into 2.5 cm (1 inch) pieces
6-8 dried Chinese mushrooms,
    soaked for 20 minutes, drained,
    stemmed and quartered
1 teaspoon salt
1 teaspoon sugar
1 teaspoon soy sauce
1 teaspoon sesame oil

Preparation time: 10 minutes,
    plus soaking
Cooking time: 3 minutes

1. Heat the oil in a wok, add the cabbage and mushrooms and stir-fry until soft.
2. Add the salt, sugar and soy sauce and cook for about 1½ minutes more. Finally add sesame oil and serve.

Chicken Noodle Soup

225 g (8 oz) chicken breast, skinned
    and cut into thin strips
pinch of salt
1 egg white
1 tablespoon cornflour
350 g (12 oz) egg noodles
1.2 litres (2 pints) chicken stock
3 tablespoons lard or vegetable oil
100 g (4 oz) canned bamboo shoots,
    drained and shredded
50 g (2 oz) dried Chinese
    mushrooms, soaked for 20
    minutes, drained, stemmed and
    shredded
225 g (8 oz) spinach leaves, stems
    removed
3 spring onions, cut into 2.5 cm
    (1 inch) lengths
Sauce:
3 tablespoons soy sauce
1 tablespoon Chinese wine or dry
    sherry
1 teaspoon salt
1 teaspoon sugar
1 teaspoon sesame oil

Preparation time: 10 minutes,
    plus soaking
Cooking time: 6-7 minutes

1. Toss the chicken strips in salt, egg white and cornflour.
2. Place noodles in boiling water for about 5 minutes, drain and place in a large serving bowl. Bring the chicken stock to the boil, pour over the noodles and keep hot.
3. Heat the lard or oil in a wok, add the chicken, bamboo shoots, mushrooms, spinach and spring onions and stir-fry all together. Mix sauce ingredients together and add to the wok. Mix well. When the sauce starts to bubble, pour it over the noodles and serve.

Sweet and Sour Pork

1 kg (2 lb) belly of pork, cut into
   2.5 cm (1 inch) cubes
1 teaspoon salt
1½ tablespoons brandy (optional)
1 egg, beaten
1 tablespoon cornflour
1 tablespoon flour
600 ml (1 pint) vegetable oil
1 spring onion, cut into 2.5 cm
   (1 inch) lengths
100 g (4 oz) canned bamboo shoots,
   drained and diced
1 green pepper, cored, seeded and
   diced

Sauce:
3 tablespoons wine vinegar
3 tablespoons sugar
½ teaspoon salt
2 tablespoons tomato purée
2 tablespoons orange juice
1 tablespoon soy sauce
1 tablespoon cornflour
1 teaspoon sesame oil

**Preparation time: 15 minutes,
plus marinating
Cooking time: 10 minutes**

---

1. Mix the pork cubes with the salt and brandy and leave to marinate for 15 minutes.
2. Blend the beaten egg, cornflour and flour, add the pork cubes and turn until each cube is well coated.
3. Mix the sauce ingredients together in a bowl.
4. Heat the oil in a wok to 180°C/350°F or until a cube of bread browns in 30 seconds. Add the pork cubes and deep fry for 3 minutes, then remove and drain on paper towels. Heat the oil again until smoking, return the pork with the bamboo shoots and fry for 2 minutes or until they are golden brown. Remove and drain on paper towels.

5. Pour off the excess oil, leaving about 1 tablespoon in the bottom of the wok, and reheat. Add the spring onion and green pepper, together with the sauce. Stir until smooth, then add the pork and bamboo shoots and toss well.

Left to right: Chinese Cabbage and Mushrooms, Chicken Noodle Soup, Sweet and Sour Pork
Illustration: A barber with his equipment – a water butt, razor strap and towels, and a stool.

The Cantonese appreciate that really fresh ingredients have a special sweetness of flavour which will be destroyed by overcooking. Their favourite way to preserve this flavour is to steam the food, or poach it gently, as with Soy-Braised Chicken. Menu serves 6.

Four Precious Vegetables

4 tablespoons vegetable oil
100 g (4 oz) canned bamboo shoots,
   drained and cut into 2.5 cm
   (1 inch) pieces
100 g (4 oz) carrots, peeled and cut
   into rings
100 g (4 oz) fresh mushrooms, left
   whole if small or quartered
100 g (4 oz) mangetout, peas,
   french beans or broccoli florets
1 teaspoon salt
1 tablespoon sugar
1 teaspoon sesame oil

Preparation time: 10 minutes
Cooking time: 3-4 minutes

1. Heat the oil in a wok, add the bamboo shoots and carrots and stir-fry for about 1 minute.
2. Add the remaining vegetables with the salt and sugar. Stir-fry together for about 1½ minutes. Sprinkle with the sesame oil and serve hot or cold.

Kidney Soup

1 tablespoon sherry
2 teaspoons cornflour
1 pork kidney or 2 lamb's kidneys,
   skinned, cored and finely sliced
900 ml (1½ pints) beef stock
6 dried Chinese mushrooms, soaked
   for 20 minutes, drained, stemmed
   and sliced
50 g (2 oz) canned bamboo shoots,
   drained and thinly sliced
1 tablespoon soy sauce
1 teaspoon salt
1 spring onion, finely chopped

Preparation time: 10 minutes,
   plus marinating and soaking
Cooking time: about 2 minutes

1. Mix the sherry with the cornflour, and marinate the kidney slices in this for 10 minutes.
2. Pour the stock into a pan and bring to the boil. Add the kidneys, mushrooms and bamboo shoots. Stir in the soy sauce and salt and boil for about 1½ minutes. Sprinkle with the spring onion and serve hot.

Top: Four Precious Vegetables
Bottom: Kidney Soup

Cantonese Soy-Braised Chicken

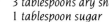

1 chicken, about 1.25 kg (2½ lb)
2 teaspoons freshly ground black pepper
2 teaspoons shredded root ginger
5 tablespoons dark soy sauce
3 tablespoons dry sherry
1 tablespoon sugar
3 tablespoons vegetable oil
100 ml (3½ fl oz) chicken stock
1 lettuce

Preparation time: 10 minutes, plus marinating
Cooking time: 50 minutes

1. Rub the inside and outside of the chicken with the pepper and ginger. Mix together the soy sauce, sherry and sugar, pour over the chicken and leave to marinate for about 20 minutes, turning the chicken occasionally.
2. Heat the oil in a wok and brown the chicken all over. Pour in the marinade liquid mixed with the chicken stock and simmer over low heat, covered, for 45 minutes. Turn occasionally, handling it with care.
3. To serve, chop into small pieces on the bone and arrange neatly on a bed of lettuce leaves. Pour a little of the sauce over the chicken.

Prawns and Green Peas

450 g (1 lb) uncooked prawns, peeled and deveined
1 egg white
2 tablespoons cornflour
3 tablespoons vegetable oil
1 slice root ginger, finely chopped
1 spring onion, finely chopped
225 g (8 oz) green peas
1½ teaspoons salt
2 teaspoons sugar
1 tablespoon dry sherry
1 teaspoon sesame oil

Preparation time: 10 minutes, plus marinating
Cooking time: 5 minutes

1. Mix the prawns with the egg white and cornflour. Leave to marinate for 10 minutes.
2. Heat the oil in a wok until smoking and add the prawns. Stir-fry for 1 minute, then remove and drain.
3. Reheat the wok and put in the ginger, spring onion and green peas. Stir together, then put in the prawns to reheat. Finally add the salt, sugar and sherry. Bring to the boil, add the sesame oil and serve immediately.

Left: Cantonese Soy-Braised Chicken
Right: Prawns and Green Peas
Illustration: A pedlar and a tobacco seller.

A meal for 4–6, ideal for those who love seafood. Because of the long South-East coastline seafood is plentiful and is often found served with noodles. The scallops, flavoured with a savoury black bean sauce, make an interesting and unusual starter.

South Sea Noodles

  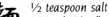

300 g (12 oz) rice noodles
6 tablespoons vegetable oil
2 medium onions, finely sliced
4 rashers bacon, cut into matchstick
   strips
2 tablespoons dried shrimps, soaked
   for 20 minutes, and drained
1 tablespoon curry powder
½ teaspoon salt
100 ml (3½ fl oz) chicken stock
2 garlic cloves, crushed
225 g (8 oz) uncooked prawns,
   peeled and deveined
1 tablespoon soy sauce
1½ tablespoons hoisin sauce
1 tablespoon dry sherry
2 spring onions, cut into 1 cm
   (½ inch) pieces
2 tablespoons chopped parsley

Preparation time: 20 minutes
Cooking time: 10 minutes

1. Blanch the noodles in boiling water for 2 minutes, refresh under cold running water and drain.
2. Heat 4 tablespoons of the oil in a wok until smoking, and add the onion, bacon and dried shrimps. Stir-fry for 1 minute, then add the curry powder and salt and fry for another minute. Pour on the stock and bring to the boil then add the noodles. Toss together until the noodles are coated with the sauce. Transfer to a heated serving dish.
3. Re-heat the wok and add the remaining oil. When the oil is hot, add the garlic and prawns. Stir-fry for 1 minute, then add the soy sauce, hoisin sauce and sherry. Pour the sauce onto the noodles, sprinkle on the spring onions and parsley and serve immediately.

Fluffy Asparagus Soup with Beef Slices

1 × 75 g (3 oz) can asparagus,
   drained and liquid reserved
1 litre (1¾ pints) chicken stock
1½ tablespoons Chinese wine or dry
   sherry
2 teaspoons salt
1 teaspoon MSG
3 tablespoons cornflour
3 tablespoons water
75 g (3 oz) fillet steak, cut into thin
   slices
pinch of freshly ground white pepper
2 egg whites

Preparation time: 10 minutes
Cooking time: 7 minutes

1. Cut the asparagus stalks into 2.5 cm (1 inch) sections.
2. Heat the stock, 1 tablespoon Chinese wine, 1½ teaspoons salt and the MSG in a large pan. Add the reserved liquid from the asparagus and bring to the boil.
3. Blend together 2 tablespoons of the cornflour with the water and stir into the soup to thicken it.
4. Mix together the remaining wine, salt, cornflour and white pepper and coat the beef slices with this mixture. Add the beef slices and asparagus pieces to the soup. Bring back to the boil, then pour on the egg whites in a thin stream. Serve immediately.

Steamed Scallops in Black Bean Sauce

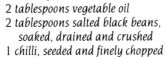

駅
汁
蒸
帯
子

12 scallops, on their shells
2 tablespoons vegetable oil
2 tablespoons salted black beans,
 soaked, drained and crushed
1 chilli, seeded and finely chopped
1 garlic clove, crushed
2 spring onions, finely chopped
2 tablespoons soy sauce
2 teaspoons sugar
3 tablespoons chicken stock
2 teaspoons cornflour

Preparation time: 5 minutes
Cooking time: 8 minutes

1. Steam the scallops on their shells for 5-6 minutes.
2. Heat the oil in a wok and add the black beans, chilli, garlic and spring onions. Stir together, then add the soy sauce, sugar and chicken stock blended with the cornflour. Stir until thickened and pour over the hot scallops. Serve immediately.

Top left: South Sea Noodles. Bottom left: Fluffy Asparagus Soup with Beef Slices. Below: Steamed Scallops in Black Bean Sauce
Illustration: Paper-making.

The food in this region is noted for its savoury quality. Oyster sauce, shrimp sauce and shrimp paste are used more widely here than anywhere else in China. Menu serves 6.

Hainan Chicken Rice

450 g (1 lb) rice
1.5 kg (3 lb) chicken, cut into 5 cm
    (2 inch) pieces
3 slices root ginger
2 medium onions, finely chopped
3 teaspoons salt
2 chicken stock cubes
275 g (10 oz) broccoli, cut into
    bite-sized pieces
100 g (4 oz) green peas

**Preparation time: 15 minutes
Cooking time: about 1 hour
    20 minutes**

1. Wash the rice, place in a pan with an equal volume of water and bring to the boil. Boil for about 6 minutes, then turn off the heat, cover and leave to steam until all the water has been absorbed.
2. Put the chicken pieces in a casserole with 1.5 litres (2½ pints) of water. Add the ginger, onion and salt. Bring to the boil, cover and simmer for 50 minutes.
3. Remove the chicken pieces and discard the ginger. Skim off the fat from the stock and add the stock cubes, broccoli, and peas. Bring to the boil, then add the rice. Cook gently for 10-12 minutes or until all the stock has been absorbed.
4. Arrange the chicken pieces on top of the rice, and put the lid back on to heat the chicken through. Serve the chicken rice from the casserole.

Fried Lettuce

1 large cos lettuce
2-3 tablespoons vegetable oil
1 teaspoon salt
1 teaspoon sugar

**Preparation time: 5 minutes
Cooking time: 2 minutes**

1. Discard the tough outer leaves and wash the lettuce well. Tear the larger leaves into 2-3 pieces, shaking off the excess water.
2. Heat the oil in a wok or large pan, then add the salt followed by the lettuce leaves and stir vigorously.
3. Add the sugar and continue to stir. As soon as the leaves become slightly limp quickly transfer them to a serving dish. Serve immediately.

Stir-Fried Beef with Oyster Sauce

350 g (12 oz) lean beef, thinly sliced
    and cut into 2.5 cm (1 inch)
    squares
4 tablespoons Chinese wine or dry
    sherry
1 tablespoon soy sauce
1 teaspoon salt
pinch of baking powder
pinch of freshly ground black pepper
1 tablespoon water
2 teaspoons sugar
2 teaspoons cornflour
600 ml (1 pint) vegetable oil
225 g (8 oz) broccoli, divided into
    florets

2 tablespoons oyster sauce
2 teaspoons finely chopped spring
    onion

**Preparation time: 15 minutes,
    plus marinating
Cooking time: 3-4 minutes**

1. Place the beef pieces in a bowl with the wine, soy sauce, ½ teaspoon salt, baking powder, pepper, water, 1 teaspoon sugar, the cornflour and 2 tablespoons vegetable oil. Leave to marinate for at least 30 minutes.

2. Cook the broccoli or spring greens in boiling water for about 2 minutes. Refresh in cold water and drain.
3. Heat the remaining oil in a wok until it is smoking, then add the beef pieces. Stir-fry for 20 seconds, removing the beef as soon as it changes colour. Drain on paper towels.
4. Pour off all but 4 tablespoons of the oil from the wok. Add the broccoli and stir-fry over high heat for 30 seconds. Add the beef, sprinkle with the oyster sauce and chopped spring onion, stir-fry for a few more seconds, then remove and serve.

Top: Hainan Chicken Rice. Bottom left:
Fried Lettuce
Bottom right: Stir-Fried Beef with Oyster
Sauce

Illustration: Dyeing silk.

Steaming, which helps to preserve the flavour of the food, is popular in this region. If possible use a fresh chicken for this Steamed Chicken dish — it will have much more flavour. The Chinese admire the pure white colour of poached or steamed chicken. If Chinese sausages are unavailable for the Egg Fried Rice, use a good Continental sausage. Menu serves 4.

Steamed Chicken with Chinese Mushrooms

450 g (1 lb) chicken breast, diced
1 teaspoon salt
½ teaspoon MSG
1 tablespoon Chinese wine or dry sherry
1 teaspoon sugar
2 teaspoons cornflour
4 dried Chinese mushrooms, soaked for 20 minutes, drained, stemmed and shredded
2 slices root ginger, peeled and shredded
1 teaspoon sesame oil
1 teaspoon Szechuan peppercorns, ground

Preparation time: 10 minutes, plus soaking
Cooking time: 20 minutes

1. In a bowl, mix together the chicken pieces, salt, MSG, wine, sugar and cornflour.
2. Place the mixture in a lightly oiled ovenproof dish. Mix together the mushrooms, ginger, sesame oil and peppercorns and spread on top of the chicken.
3. Place the dish in a steamer, cover and steam vigorously for 20 minutes. Serve hot.

Chinese Sausage and Egg Fried Rice

3 tablespoons vegetable oil
1 teaspoon salt
2 eggs, lightly beaten
100 g (4 oz) Chinese sausages, sliced
450 g (1 lb) cooked rice
½ teaspoon MSG
½ teaspoon finely ground black pepper
100 g (4 oz) petits pois
4 spring onions, finely chopped

Preparation time: 15 minutes
Cooking time: 10 minutes

1. Heat a wok over high heat for about 30 seconds, then add 1 tablespoon vegetable oil. When the oil is hot, add ½ teaspoon of salt, then the eggs. Stir-fry until the eggs are set, then transfer them to a bowl.
2. Add 2 tablespoons of oil to the wok and allow it to heat. Add the Chinese sausages and stir-fry for about one minute, then add the rice, ½ teaspoon salt, MSG and pepper. Stir-fry for a few more minutes, then add the petits pois and spring onions.
3. Stir continuously for 2-3 minutes until the rice is well flavoured. Stir in the eggs, then transfer the mixture to a hot serving dish.

Prawns Fu Yung

225 g (8 oz) uncooked prawns, peeled and deveined
1 slice root ginger, finely chopped
1 teaspoon cornflour
6 eggs, beaten
1 teaspoon salt
1 spring onion, finely chopped
3 tablespoons vegetable oil
1 tablespoon Chinese wine or dry sherry

Preparation time: 10 minutes
Cooking time: 5 minutes

1. Mix the prawns with the ginger root and cornflour.
2. Beat the eggs in a bowl with the salt and add the spring onion.
3. Heat a wok with 1 tablespoon of the oil until it begins to smoke. Add the prawns and stir-fry for about 1 minute. Add the wine to the wok and then pour the prawn mixture into the egg and spring onion mixture.
4. Add the remaining oil to the wok. Reheat, then add the prawn and egg mixture. Stir gently to scramble for a few minutes, and serve before the egg sets too hard.

> Chinese sausages make a very useful standby. They are usually available in Chinese supermarkets. These sausages keep well for a month in the refrigerator or indefinitely in the freezer.

Top: Steamed Chicken with Chinese Mushrooms
Bottom left: Chinese Sausage and Egg Fried Rice
Bottom right: Prawns Fu Yung

Illustration: China shop with cash desk.

The duck and the crab are both classic Cantonese dishes, ideal for this dinner party menu for a special occasion. Don't forget to provide finger bowls and extra napkins in case your guests want to eat the crab with their fingers, as the Chinese do. In spite of the long list of ingredients the duck is very easy to prepare. Menu serves 6–8.

Boneless Duck with Eight Precious Stuffing

1 duck gizzard (optional)
2 tablespoons vegetable oil
4 spring onions, finely chopped
2 slices root ginger, peeled and finely chopped
4 dried Chinese mushrooms, soaked for 20 minutes, drained, stemmed and diced
20 dried lotus seeds soaked overnight, drained and diced
15 g (½ oz) dried shrimps, soaked for 20 minutes, drained and chopped

100 g (4 oz) cooked ham, diced
8 dried chestnuts, soaked overnight, simmered until soft and chopped
2 tablespoons Chinese wine or dry sherry
2 tablespoons light soy sauce
½ teaspoon salt
freshly ground black pepper
450 g (1 lb) glutinous rice, cooked
1 duck, about 1.5 kg (3½ lb), boned (ask the butcher to do this)
2 tablespoons dark soy sauce

Preparation time: 20 minutes, plus soaking
Cooking time: about 1 hour 15 minutes
Oven: 190°C, 375°F, Gas Mark 5

1. Boil the duck gizzard, if using, for 10 minutes, then drain and dice.
2. Heat the oil in a wok until smoking and add half of the spring onions and the ginger. Stir together for a few

seconds, then add the mushrooms, duck gizzard, lotus seeds, shrimps, diced ham, chestnuts, wine, light soy sauce, salt and pepper. Mix together well, add the rice and mix again.

3. Pack this mixture into the duck and reform the shape. Do not stuff too full. Close up the tail and neck openings with a needle and thread.

4. Wipe the duck dry and brush with the dark soy sauce. Place on a wire tray over a roasting tin and roast in the preheated oven for 1¼ hours or until the juices run clear.

5. To serve, make a long central cut down the breast and sprinkle with remaining spring onions.

Left: Boneless Duck with Eight Precious Stuffing
Top right: Braised Broccoli
Bottom right: Ginger and Spring Onion Crab

Braised Broccoli or Cauliflower

3 tablespoons vegetable oil
450 g (1 lb) broccoli or cauliflower, divided into florets
1 teaspoon salt
1 teaspoon sugar
4 tablespoons chicken stock or water

Preparation time: 5 minutes
Cooking time: 2 minutes

1. Heat the oil in a wok, add the broccoli and stir-fry for about 1 minute, then add salt, sugar and stock.
2. Cook for 2-3 minutes at most, stirring a few times during cooking. Serve hot.

Ginger and Spring Onion Crab

1 boiled crab, about 1.25 kg (2¾ lb), cleaned and chopped through the shell into large bite-sized pieces
3 tablespoons sherry
3 tablespoons soy sauce
2 tablespoons cornflour
4 tablespoons vegetable oil
4 slices root ginger, peeled and finely chopped
4 spring onions, finely chopped
1 teaspoon salt
2 teaspoons sugar

Preparation time: 20 minutes
Cooking time: 7 minutes

1. Place the crab pieces in a bowl, add 2 tablespoons sherry, 2 tablespoons soy sauce and the cornflour. Turn the pieces until well coated.
2. Heat the oil in a wok until smoking, then add the crab and fry for about 1 minute. Add the ginger, spring onions, salt, remaining soy sauce, sugar and the remaining sherry. Stir-fry on high heat for about 3 minutes, stirring all the time. Add a little water if the mixture becomes very dry.
3. Transfer the crab pieces to a warm serving dish and pour over the sauce.

Pomegranate Crispy Prawn Balls, studded with croûtons, make an attractive and unusual starter, while the chicken dish has a lovely fresh lemony taste. Served with the spring greens, it needs only rice to make a well rounded meal, ideal for a lunch party. This menu serves 4.

Stir-Fried Spring Greens with Garlic

450 g (1 lb) tender spring greens, washed and drained
1 teaspoon salt
4 tablespoons vegetable oil
2 teaspoons chopped garlic
½ teaspoon sugar
1 tablespoon water

Preparation time: 10 minutes, plus soaking
Cooking time: 3 minutes

1. Cut the spring greens into 2.5 cm (1 inch) lengths. Cover with water, add the salt, and leave to soak for 10 minutes. Drain thoroughly.
2. Heat the oil in a wok until smoking. Add the garlic, stir-fry for a few seconds to flavour the oil, then add the greens, sugar and water. Stir-fry for 1-2 minutes, until the colour changes to transparent green. Transfer to a hot serving dish and serve.

Fried Chicken Slices in Lemon Sauce

350 g (12 oz) chicken breast, cut into 2.5 cm (1 inch) slices
1 teaspoon salt
1 tablespoon Chinese wine or dry sherry
½ tablespoon light soy sauce
2 tablespoons cornflour
4 tablespoons chicken stock
1 egg yolk
pinch of freshly ground white pepper
3 tablespoons plain flour
600 ml (1 pint) vegetable oil
3 tablespoons sugar
3 tablespoons fresh lemon juice
1 teaspoon sesame oil
lemon slices and rind, to garnish

Preparation time: 20 minutes, plus marinating
Cooking time: 15 minutes

'Pomegranate' Crispy Prawn Balls

酥炸百花蝦球

4 slices white bread, crusts removed
    and cut into 1 cm (½ inch) cubes
225 g (8 oz) white fish fillets, minced
225 g (8 oz) uncooked prawns, peeled,
    deveined and minced
2 teaspoons salt
pinch of freshly ground white pepper
2 egg whites, lightly beaten
2 tablespoons cornflour
2 slices root ginger, peeled and finely
    chopped
600 ml (1 pint) vegetable oil
lettuce leaves, to serve

Preparation time: 20 minutes
Cooking time: 10 minutes

1. Mix the chicken pieces in a bowl with half the salt, the wine, soy sauce, 1 tablespoon cornflour, 1 tablespoon chicken stock, egg yolk and white pepper. Marinate for about 10 minutes.
2. Dust the chicken pieces with the plain flour. Heat the oil in a wok to 180°C/350°F or until a cube of bread browns in 30 seconds. Add the chicken and deep-fry until golden brown, about 1 minute. Remove and drain on paper towels.
3. Pour off all but 1 tablespoon of the oil from the wok and reheat. Add the sugar, lemon juice, remaining salt, sesame oil and cornflour blended with the remaining chicken stock to thicken the sauce. Pour the sauce over the chicken slices and serve, garnished with lemon slices and then strips of lemon rind.

1. Toast the bread cubes lightly until light brown and dry.
2. Mix together the minced fish, prawns, salt, pepper, egg whites, cornflour and finely chopped ginger. Form the mixture into balls, using about 1 tablespoon per ball, then roll each ball in the croûtons until coated.
3. Heat the oil in a wok to 180°C/350°F or until a cube of bread browns in 30 seconds. Gently lower the balls into the oil and deep-fry until light brown. Remove and drain on paper towels. Serve as an hors d'oeuvre or starter, on a bed of lettuce leaves.

Left to right: Stir-Fried Spring Greens with Garlic, Fried Chicken Slices in Lemon Sauce, Pomegranate Crispy Prawn Balls

A spectacular menu which is sure to impress everyone. The intriguing little cellophane parcels are unwrapped to reveal beef slices deliciously flavoured with mango. Wrapping food in cellophane paper is popular in deep-frying and helps to seal in the flavour. (After unwrapping, the paper is discarded.) Serves 4-6.

Red-Cooked Fish

紅燒魚

1 carp, sea bass, mullet or mackerel, about 750 g (1½ lb)
1 tablespoon dark soy sauce
3 tablespoons vegetable oil
15 g (½ oz) wood ears, soaked for 20 minutes, and drained
50 g (2 oz) canned bamboo shoots, drained and sliced
3 spring onions, shredded
3 slices root ginger, shredded
2 teaspoons cornflour
1 tablespoon water
Sauce:
2 tablespoons dark soy sauce
2 tablespoons Chinese wine or dry sherry
2 teaspoons sugar
4 tablespoons beef stock

Preparation time: 10 minutes, plus marinating and soaking
Cooking time: 15 minutes

1. Make diagonal cuts down both sides of the fish. Rub with the soy sauce and leave to marinate for 15 minutes.
2. Heat the oil in a wok until it smokes, add the fish and fry on both sides until golden. Add the ready-mixed sauce together with the wood ears and bamboo shoots and continue cooking gently for about 10 minutes. Add the spring onions and ginger. When the sauce has reduced by half, stir in the cornflour blended with the water, turn the fish over once, then serve.

Top: Stir-Fried Minced Chicken on Crispy Rice Noodles
Bottom: Red-Cooked Fish

Stir-Fried Minced Chicken on Crispy Rice Noodles

炒
鸡
鬆

225 g (8 oz) chicken meat, minced
1½ teaspoons salt
2 tablespoons cornflour
1 tablespoon water
300 ml (½ pint) vegetable oil
75 g (3 oz) rice noodles
2 eggs, beaten lightly
3 dried Chinese mushrooms, soaked
    for 20 minutes, drained, stemmed
    and diced
3 slices of cooked ham, diced
50 g (2 oz) canned bamboo shoots,
    drained and diced
100 g (4 oz) green beans, diced
1 tablespoon soy sauce
1 teaspoon sesame oil
2 tablespoons chicken stock
pinch of freshly ground white pepper
½ teaspoon sugar
3 spring onions, chopped
20 pancakes (see page 47)

**Preparation time: 40 minutes,
    including marinating and
    soaking
Cooking time: 15 minutes**

1. Mix the chicken with ½ teaspoon salt, 1 tablespoon cornflour and the water. Marinate for 20 minutes.
2. Heat the oil in a wok to 180°C/ 350°F or until a cube of bread browns in 30 seconds. Put in the rice noodles – they should puff up immediately. Remove from the wok and drain.
3. Reheat the oil until it is smoking, and add the chicken. Deep-fry for 30 seconds and then lift out and drain.
4. Heat a lightly oiled crêpe pan, pour in the beaten eggs and cook until lightly browned underneath. Turn the omelette and cook gently on the other side. Lift out the omelette and cut into short, narrow strips.
5. Pour off all but 3 tablespoons of the oil. Reheat the wok, then add the mushrooms, ham, bamboo shoots and green beans and stir-fry for 1 minute. Add the chicken, omelette strips, remaining salt, cornflour, soy sauce, sesame oil, chicken stock, white pepper and sugar. Bring to the boil, stirring until thickened, then add the spring onions. Arrange the rice noodles on a warmed serving dish and pour on the chicken mixture. Serve with pancakes.

Mango Beef in Paper

纸
包
芒
果
牛
肉

225 g (8 oz) fillet steak, cut into
    12 slices
1 tablespoon oyster sauce
pinch of salt
2 teaspoons cornflour
1 tablespoon sugar
½ teaspoon sesame oil
pinch of freshly ground white pepper
12 thin slices root ginger, peeled
1 mango, stoned and cut into
    12 slices
2 spring onions, cut into 12 pieces
1 sheet cellophane, cut into
    12 squares, or 12 small oven
    roasting bags
600 ml (1 pint) vegetable oil
lettuce leaves, to serve

**Preparation time: 10 minutes,
    plus marinating
Cooking time: 4–6 minutes**

1. Place the beef slices in a bowl with the oyster sauce, salt, cornflour, sugar, sesame oil and white pepper. Leave to marinate for 10 minutes.
2. Place a slice of beef on each sheet of cellophane. Top with a slice of ginger and a piece of spring onion and finish with a slice of mango. Wrap up the cellophane to form an airtight parcel, or tie roasting bag at the top.
3. Heat the oil in a wok to 180°C/ 350°F, or until a cube of bread browns in 30 seconds, and put in the parcels. Deep-fry for about 2 minutes on each side, depending on how you like your steak, then remove and drain on paper towels.
4. Serve immediately on lettuce leaves.

Mango Beef in Paper, served with Cantonese Fried Rice (page 110)

An easy, trouble-free way of cooking poultry is to bury the whole bird in sea salt and then bake it. In spite of what you might think, the flesh does *not* taste salty, and the salt absorbs the fat and moisture from the skin during cooking, leaving the outside dry and crisp. The salt can be kept and re-used. With rice or noodles, this menu will serve 5–6.

Sweet and Sour Spare Ribs

750 g (1½ lb) spare ribs, cut into 5 cm (2 inch) pieces (ask the butcher to do this for you)
4 tablespoons Chinese wine or dry sherry
3 tablespoons soy sauce
3½ tablespoons cornflour
600 ml (1 pint) vegetable oil
2 teaspoons chopped spring onion
2 teaspoons chopped root ginger
1 garlic clove, crushed
3 tablespoons sugar
3 tablespoons wine vinegar
1 tablespoon soy sauce
2 tablespoons tomato ketchup
4-5 tablespoons water

Preparation time: 20 minutes, plus marinating
Cooking time: 10 minutes

1. Place the spare ribs in a bowl with the wine and 3 tablespoons soy sauce and leave to marinate for 20 minutes.
2. Toss the marinated spare ribs in 3 tablespoons cornflour. Heat the oil in a wok, put in the spare ribs and cook over medium heat for 2 minutes, then remove and drain on paper towels. Reheat oil until smoking, return the spare ribs to the wok and deep-fry again for 5 seconds. Remove and drain on paper towels.
3. Pour off all but 2 tablespoons of the oil and reheat. Add the remaining marinade, chopped spring onion, ginger and garlic and stir-fry for 1 minute. Add the sugar, vinegar, remaining soy sauce, tomato ketchup, remaining cornflour and water and bring to the boil. Place the spare ribs in this sauce and mix well. Serve immediately.

Crispy 'Seaweed'

干
貝
鬆

1 kg (2 lb) spring greens, shaved into very fine shreds
600 ml (1 pint) vegetable oil
1½ teaspoons caster sugar
½ teaspoon salt
pinch of MSG
50 g (2 oz) flaked almonds

Preparation time: 20 minutes, plus draining
Cooking time: 2½ minutes

1. Wash the spring green shavings and dry thoroughly by spreading them out on paper towels and draining for about 30 minutes (they must be completely dry).
2. Heat the oil in a wok until smoking, then remove from the heat and add the spring green shavings. Stir and return the wok to the heat. Stir-fry for 2½ minutes. Remove and drain. Arrange on a serving dish.
3. Sprinkle evenly with the sugar, salt, MSG and almonds.

Top: Sweet and Sour Spare Ribs
Right: Crispy 'Seaweed', East River Salt-Buried Chicken
Illustration: The Emperor of China approaches his tent.

East River Salt-Buried Chicken

1.5-1.75 kg (3-4 lb) chicken
1½ tablespoons Rose Dew liqueur or fruit-flavoured brandy
1½ tablespoons soy sauce
4 slices root ginger, shredded
1 large onion, finely sliced
1 tablespoon whole, mixed 5-spice
2.75-3 kg (6-7 lb) coarse sea salt

Preparation time: 15 minutes, plus marinating
Cooking time: about 1½ hours
Oven: 180°C, 350°F, Gas Mark 4

1. Rub the chicken inside and out with a mixture of the Rose Dew liqueur and the soy sauce. Mix together the ginger, onion and 5-spice and place inside the chicken. Leave to marinate for 2-3 hours.

2. Pour a layer of the salt into a deep casserole dish. Place the chicken on top then pour in sea salt to completely cover the chicken. Cover and place over low heat for 10 minutes, then place in a preheated oven for 1½ hours.

3. To serve, lift the chicken out of the casserole and brush free of salt. Chop through the bone into 20-24 pieces and serve on a heated serving dish.

Wrapping food is a wonderful way to seal in the flavours. Fish wrapped and steamed in this way has a fresh juiciness – Chinese restaurants keep fish alive in tanks until they are ready for cooking. Unwrap the fish at the table – it should be tender enough to eat with chopsticks. Serves 4-6.

Spare Ribs in Yellow Bean Paste

450 g (1 lb) spare ribs, cut into 5 cm (2 inch) pieces (ask the butcher to do this for you)
1 tablespoon soy sauce
2 tablespoons Chinese wine or dry sherry
1 tablespoon sugar
1 tablespoon flour
300 ml (½ pint) vegetable oil
1 garlic clove, crushed
2 spring onions, cut into 2.5 cm (1 inch) lengths
2 tablespoons yellow bean paste
1 small green pepper, cored, seeded and sliced
1 small red pepper, cored, seeded and sliced

Preparation time: 10 minutes, plus marinating
Cooking time: 30 minutes

1. Mix the spare ribs with soy sauce, wine, sugar and flour and leave to marinate for 10-15 minutes.
2. Heat the oil in a wok to 180°C/350°F or until a cube of bread browns in 30 seconds. Add the spare-ribs and fry until golden. Remove and drain on paper towels. Pour off all but 1 tablespoon of this oil and reheat.
3. Put in the garlic, spring onions and yellow bean paste. Stir for a few minutes, then put in the spare ribs, blend well, add a little stock or water, cover and cook over high heat for 5 minutes, adding a little more stock or water if necessary. Replace the lid and cook for a further 5 minutes or so, finally add the green and red peppers, stir a few more times and serve hot.

Paper-Wrapped Fried Chicken

450 g (1 lb) chicken breast, thinly sliced and cut into 5 cm (2 inch) squares
3 tablespoons soy sauce
½ teaspoon sugar
½ teaspoon salt
1 tablespoon Chinese wine or dry sherry
1 tablespoon cornflour
pinch of freshly ground black pepper
15 sheets of cellophane, measuring 10 × 10 cm (4 × 4 inches) or 15 small roasting bags
2 tablespoons sesame oil
15 small coriander sprigs
4 dried Chinese mushrooms, soaked for 20 minutes, drained, stemmed and quartered
2 slices of cooked ham, cut into similar-sized pieces as the mushrooms
1.2 litres (2 pints) vegetable oil

Preparation time: 20 minutes, plus marinating and soaking
Cooking time: 10 minutes

Left: Spare Ribs in Yellow Bean Paste
Right: Paper-Wrapped Fried Chicken

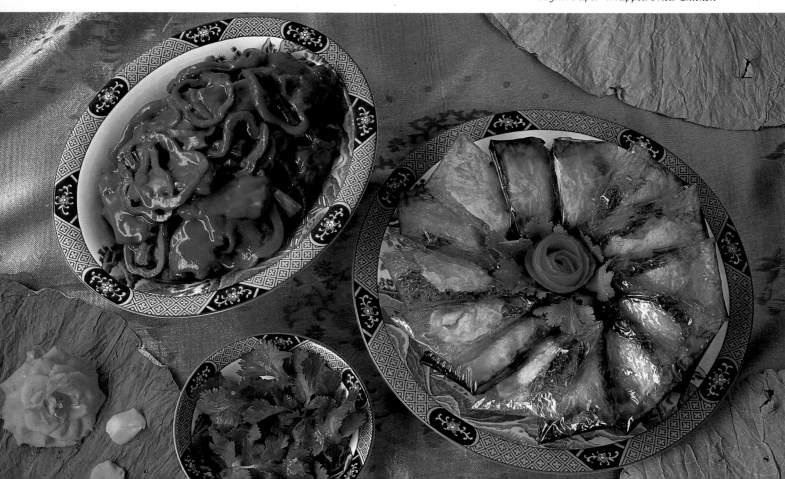

1. Place the chicken pieces in a bowl with the soy sauce, sugar, salt, wine, cornflour and black pepper and toss well. Leave to marinate for about 10 minutes.

2. Brush the cellophane sheets or oven bags with sesame oil. Lay on each sheet a sprig of coriander, a piece of mushroom, ham and a slice of chicken. Fold up the cellophane to seal or tie oven bag at the top.

3. Heat the oil to 180°C/350°F or until a cube of bread browns in 30 seconds. Carefully lower the parcels into the oil and deep-fry for about 2 minutes. Serve straight out of the paper.

Fish Wrapped in Lotus Leaves

1 mullet, sea-bass, carp or trout, about 1.25 kg (2½ lb)
2 tablespoons soy sauce
1 teaspoon salt
2 tablespoons hoisin sauce
2 tablespoons vegetable oil
2 tablespoons Chinese wine or dry sherry
3 slices root ginger, shredded
3 spring onions, finely chopped
2 lotus leaves
stuffing:
1½ tablespoons lard
2 onions, finely chopped
2 rashers bacon, finely shredded
100 g (4 oz) mushrooms, quartered

Preparation time: 15 minutes, plus marinating
Cooking time: 45 minutes steaming or 50 minutes baking
Oven: 200°C, 400°F, Gas Mark 6, then 160°C, 325°F, Gas Mark 2

1. Wash and dry the fish. Mix together the soy sauce, salt, hoisin sauce, oil and wine. Rub the fish inside and out with the mixture and leave to marinate for 30 minutes.

2. Heat a wok, add the lard and stir until it melts. Add the onions, bacon and mushrooms and stir-fry for 1½ minutes. Remove from the wok and drain on paper towels.

3. Remove the fish from the marinade and stuff with the onion mixture. Wrap carefully in the lotus leaves, then wrap a sheet of foil round to keep the leaves in place.

4. Steam vigorously for 45 minutes, or bake in a preheated oven for 25 minutes, then reduce heat and bake for another 25 minutes.

5. Serve the fish wrapped in lotus leaves and unwrap the fish at the table for everyone to help themselves.

Above, Fish Wrapped in Lotus Leaves

Prawns are plentiful and can be found served in many different ways. These king prawns, stuffed and decorated with finely shredded vegetables, make a colourful starter. The tails are left on so that they can be easily picked up and eaten with the fingers. Squid flowers are made by scoring the fish with a criss-cross pattern before cutting it into squares or strips. When placed in hot oil, the pieces open up. Menu serves 4–5.

Beef Steak Cantonese Style

2 slices root ginger, peeled and finely
　　chopped
3 spring onions, finely chopped
1 tablespoon Chinese wine or dry
　　sherry
7 tablespoons water
pinch of freshly ground white pepper
2 tablespoons soy sauce
450 g (1 lb) fillet steak, cut across
　　the grain into 5 mm (¼ inch)
　　thick slices
600 ml (1 pint) vegetable oil
1 tablespoon plain flour
1½ tablespoons cornflour
225 g (8 oz) mangetout
½ teaspoon salt
1 tablespoon tomato ketchup
1 tablespoon Worcestershire sauce
2 tablespoons sugar

**Preparation time: 10 minutes,
　plus marinating
Cooking time: 4-5 minutes**

1. Mix together the ginger, half the spring onions, the wine, 4 tablespoons of water, white pepper and 1 tablespoon soy sauce. Add the beef slices, mix well together and leave to marinate for 15-20 minutes.
2. Heat the oil in a wok to 180°C/ 350°F or until a cube of bread browns in 30 seconds. Mix together the plain

flour and half the cornflour. Remove the beef from the marinade, dust with the flour and deep-fry for about 30 seconds. Remove from the oil and drain on paper towels.
3. Pour off most of the oil from the wok, leaving about 1 tablespoon. Reheat the wok, and add the salt and mangetout. Stir-fry for about 1½ minutes then remove and arrange in a ring on a serving dish.
4. Heat another tablespoon of oil in the wok and add the remaining soy sauce, the tomato ketchup, Worcestershire sauce and sugar. Blend the remaining cornflour with the remaining water and add to the wok to thicken the sauce. Bring to the boil then add the beef slices. Toss the slices until coated with the sauce, then arrange in the middle of the mangetout ring. Sprinkle with the remaining spring onions and serve.

Squid Flowers and Green Peppers

青

椒

鮮

魷

450 g (1 lb) squid, cleaned and head
   removed
600 ml (1 pint) vegetable oil
2 slices root ginger, peeled and finely
   chopped
225 g (8 oz) green peppers, cored,
   seeded and cut into 4 cm
   (1½ inch) pieces
1 teaspoon salt
1 tablespoon soy sauce
1 teaspoon wine vinegar
freshly ground black pepper
1 teaspoon sesame oil

Preparation time: 20 minutes
Cooking time: 10 minutes

1. Open up the squid and cut a criss-cross pattern on the inside with a sharp knife. Cut the squid into 4 cm (1½ inch) squares.
2. Heat the oil in a wok to 180°C/350°F or until a cube of bread browns in 30 seconds. Quickly deep-fry the squid for about 30 seconds, then remove and drain on paper towels.
3. Pour off all but 1 tablespoon of the oil. Reheat the wok and add the ginger and green peppers. Stir together for a few seconds and then add the squid, followed by the salt, soy sauce, vinegar and pepper. Bring to the boil, sprinkle on the sesame oil and serve.

Deep-Fried King Prawns

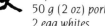

炸

大

蝦

10 uncooked king prawns, peeled
   but with the tails left on
150 g (5 oz) plain flour
225 g (8 oz) uncooked prawns,
   peeled and minced
50 g (2 oz) pork fat, minced
2 egg whites
½ teaspoon salt
2 tablespoons cornflour
1 tablespoon Chinese wine or dry
   sherry
2 slices root ginger, peeled and finely
   chopped
pinch of freshly ground white pepper
pinch of MSG
½ teaspoon sesame oil
600 ml (1 pint) vegetable oil
lettuce leaves, to serve
lemon slices, to garnish

Decoration:
1 slice cooked ham, thinly shredded
2 green beans, finely diced
1 carrot, cut into fine julienne strips

Preparation time: 30 minutes
Cooking time: 5 minutes

1. Slice the prawns down the back vein, devein and open them out flat. Dust with the plain flour.
2. In a bowl mix together the prawns, pork fat, egg whites, salt, cornflour, wine, ginger, white pepper, MSG and sesame oil.
3. Divide the mixture into 10 portions and carefully spoon each portion onto one of the flattened prawns.

4. Decorate with the ham, beans and carrot. Dust again with plain flour.
5. Heat the oil in a wok to 180°C/350°F or until a cube of bread browns in 30 seconds. Gently lower the prawns one by one into the oil. Deep-fry until golden brown and cooked through, about 3 minutes. Remove and drain on paper towels. Serve hot on a bed of lettuce leaves and garnish with lemon slices.

Clockwise from the front: Deep-Fried King Prawns, Beef Steak Cantonese Style, Squid Flowers and Green Peppers
Illustration: Monkeys picking tea.

This somewhat extravagant menu could be reserved for a very special occasion. The Quails' Eggs on Toast can be served as a starter, to be eaten with the fingers. The lobster would also be eaten with the fingers in China. Provide finger bowls and hot towels. Menu serves 6.

Cantonese Lobster

1 lobster, about 1.5 kg (3 lb), alive if possible
5 tablespoons vegetable oil
4 slices root ginger, peeled and shredded
4 spring onions, cut into 2.5 cm (1 inch) lengths
½ teaspoon salt
150 ml (¼ pint) chicken stock
1½ tablespoons soy sauce
2 tablespoons Chinese wine or dry sherry

Preparation time: 20 minutes
Cooking time: about 10 minutes

1. Kill the lobster (or ask the fishmonger to do this for you), clean it and chop through the shell into large bite-size pieces.
2. Heat the oil in a wok until it is smoking. Add the lobster pieces, cover and cook in the hot oil for 3 minutes. Lift out and drain on paper towels.
3. Add the ginger, spring onions and salt and stir in the hot oil for 1 minute. Add the stock, soy sauce and wine. Bring to the boil, stirring, then add the pieces of lobster. Turn them in the stock, and cover firmly. Leave to cook over high heat for 4 minutes, when the liquid should have reduced by about one-third. Transfer the lobster pieces to a deep-sided serving dish, pour over the sauce and serve.

Quails' Eggs on Toast with Mashed Shrimps

750 g (1½ lb) peeled shrimps, mashed to a paste
50 g (2 oz) pork fat, minced
1 teaspoon minced root ginger
1 spring onion, finely chopped
1 egg white, lightly beaten
pinch of freshly ground white pepper
2 teaspoons salt
½ teaspoon sesame oil
pinch of MSG
1 tablespoon Chinese wine or dry sherry
1½ teaspoons cornflour
2 sprigs of parsley, finely chopped
1 slice cooked ham, finely chopped
8 slices thin white bread, crusts removed and cut in half
16 quails' eggs, hard-boiled and shelled
600 ml (1 pint) vegetable oil

Preparation time: 10 minutes
Cooking time: 5 minutes

...

Yeh-Shung Shredded Pork

225 g (8 oz) pork fillet, shredded
2 egg whites
75 g (3 oz) cornflour
2 tablespoons Chinese wine or dry
  sherry
300 ml (½ pint) vegetable oil
5 cm (2 inch) piece canned bamboo
  shoot, drained and shredded
3 dried Chinese mushrooms, soaked
  for 20 minutes, drained, stemmed
  and shredded
2 spring onions, finely chopped
2 slices root ginger, finely chopped
1 garlic clove, crushed
1 chilli, seeded and finely chopped
1 teaspoon black bean paste
1 teaspoon salt
1 teaspoon dark soy sauce
1 teaspoon wine vinegar

½ teaspoon freshly ground white
  pepper
1 tablespoon chicken stock
½ teaspoon sesame oil
½ teaspoon red chilli oil
1 teaspoon Szechuan peppercorns,
  ground

**Preparation time: 15 minutes,
  plus soaking
Cooking time: 8 minutes**

1. In a bowl, mix together the shredded pork, egg whites, all but 1 teaspoon cornflour and 1 tablespoon wine.
2. Heat the oil in a wok and add the pork. Stir-fry until almost cooked (about 2 minutes), then add the bamboo shoot and mushrooms. Stir-fry together for 1 minute then remove from the oil and drain on paper towels.
3. Pour off all but 1 tablespoon of the oil and reheat the wok. Add the spring onions, ginger, garlic and chilli. Stir together and add the bean paste, remaining wine, salt, soy sauce, vinegar and white pepper. Bring to the boil and return the pork and vegetables to the wok.
4. Blend together the remaining cornflour and the chicken stock. Stir into the wok to thicken the sauce, simmer for 1 minute and then pour onto a serving dish. Sprinkle with the sesame oil, chilli oil and Szechuan peppercorns and serve.

To clean the lobster, first cut off the head and tail. Discard the stomach sac which lies in the head, the grey spongy gills which lie between the tail and the main body shell, and the intestinal vein which runs down the tail. Clean under running water then chop through the shell into large pieces.

1. In a bowl, mix together the shrimps, pork fat, ginger, spring onion, egg white, white pepper, salt, sesame oil, MSG, wine and cornflour. Beat all together until thoroughly blended.
2. Mix together the parsley and ham.
3. Divide the shrimp mixture between the 16 pieces of bread. Spread on an even layer and place a quail's egg firmly in the centre of each. Sprinkle on the ham and parsley and press into the filling.
4. Heat the oil in a wok to 180°C/350°F, or until a cube of bread browns in 30 seconds. Gently place the bread slices, filling side down, in the oil. Fry until golden brown on both sides, drain on paper towels and serve.

*Left: Cantonese Lobster. Top right: Yeh-Shung Shredded Pork
Bottom right: Quails' Eggs on Toast with Mashed Shrimps*

Ho Fan noodles are flat ribbon noodles made with rice flour. They are most popular in South China, where rice is grown in abundance, and can be bought fresh in this country in Chinese supermarkets. If unobtainable, use dried noodles and cook for 10-12 minutes or until tender. Serve the colourful Prawn Balls as a starter. Menu serves 5–6.

Black Bean Beef with Ho Fan Noodles

1 teaspoon salt
pinch of freshly ground white pepper
1½ tablespoons cornflour
1 egg white
450 g (1 lb) beef steak, cut into
    2.5 cm (1 inch) slices
4 tablespoons vegetable oil
2 large onions, sliced into rings
2 tablespoons salted black beans,
    soaked, drained and crushed
1½ tablespoons soy sauce
2 tablespoons hoisin sauce
4 tablespoons chicken stock
450 g (1 lb) fresh ho fan noodles,
    boiled for 1 minute and drained
1 tablespoon chopped spring onions

Preparation time: 5 minutes,
    plus marinating and soaking
Cooking time: 10 minutes

1. Mix together the salt, pepper, 1 tablespoon cornflour and the egg white. Marinate the beef slices in the mixture for 15 minutes.
2. Heat the oil in a wok until smoking, then add the onion rings. Stir-fry for 1 minute then add the beef. Stir-fry for another minute then remove to a plate.
3. Pour off all but 1 tablespoon of the oil and reheat. Add the black beans. Stir over heat for 30 seconds then add the soy sauce, hoisin sauce and half the stock. Stir together then add the remaining cornflour blended with the remaining stock.
4. Add the noodles with the beef and onions and toss together until heated through. Sprinkle with spring onion.

Multicoloured Prawn Balls

225 g (8 oz) uncooked prawns,
    peeled, deveined and minced
50 g (2 oz) pork fat
2 egg whites
½ teaspoon salt
pinch of freshly ground white pepper
pinch of MSG
50 g (2 oz) cornflour
2 slices root ginger, peeled and finely
    chopped
1 tablespoon Chinese wine or dry
    sherry
½ teaspoon sesame oil
600 ml (1 pint) vegetable oil
lemon slices, to garnish
Coating:
2 leaves Chinese cabbage, finely
    shredded
1 carrot, scraped and finely chopped
2 radishes, peeled and skin finely
    chopped
25 g (1 oz) rice noodles, deep-fried in
    hot oil and crumbled

Preparation time: 20 minutes
Cooking time: 10 minutes

1. Mix together in a bowl the prawns, pork fat, egg whites, salt, pepper, MSG, cornflour, ginger, wine and sesame oil. Make sure it is all thoroughly mixed.
2. Roll the mixture into balls, using about 1 tablespoon of mixture per ball. Mix together all the coating ingredients in a bowl and roll each ball in this to coat thickly.
3. Heat the oil in a wok to 180°C/350°F, or until a cube of bread browns in 30 seconds. Add the prawn balls and deep-fry until they are cooked through and crisp. Garnish with thinly sliced lemon.

Left: Black Bean Beef with Ho Fan Noodles
Top right: Spare Ribs in Capital Sauce
Bottom right: Multicoloured Prawn Balls

Illustration: Making silk rope.

Spare Ribs in Capital Sauce

京都排骨

1 egg
100 g (4 oz) cornflour, plus
    1½ tablespoons
7 tablespoons water
1 kg (2¼ lb) spare ribs, cut into
    5 cm (2 inch) pieces
600 ml (1 pint) vegetable oil
2 spring onions, finely chopped
2 slices root ginger, peeled and finely
    chopped
1½ tablespoons sugar
2 tablespoons wine vinegar
1 tablespoon tomato purée
1 small onion, cut into wedges
4 dried Chinese mushrooms, soaked
    for 20 minutes, drained, stemmed
    and shredded

**Preparation time: 15 minutes,
    plus soaking
Cooking time: 8-10 minutes**

1. Make a batter with the egg, 100 g
(4 oz) cornflour and 6 tablespoons of
water. Place the spare ribs in the
batter and turn until well coated.
2. Heat the oil in a wok to 180°C/
350°F or until a cube of bread browns
in 30 seconds. Lower the spare ribs
into the oil and deep-fry until golden
brown, about 5 minutes. Remove and
drain on paper towels.
3. Pour off the oil from the wok, wipe
clean with paper towels, then reheat.
Put in the spring onions and ginger
and stir-fry together quickly. Mix
together the remaining cornflour, the
sugar, vinegar, tomato purée and remaining water. Add to the wok and
stir until thickened. Bring to the boil,
then add the onion and mushrooms
and stir for another minute.
4. Pour the sauce on top of the spare
ribs, or use as a dip.

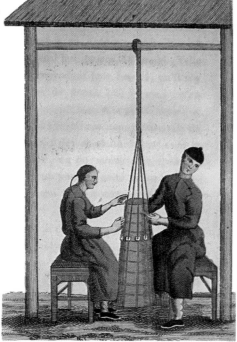

Cha Siu is the specialized form of Cantonese roasting. The meat is first marinated in a soy sauce mixture and then quick roasted at a high temperature. The high heat causes the marinade to become encrusted on the surface of the pork forming a dark rim round each slice. Menu serves 4–6.

Cha Siu Roast Pork

2 tablespoons red bean curd cheese
2 tablespoons dark soy sauce
1 tablespoon yellow bean sauce
3 teaspoons vegetable oil
2 teaspoons sugar
2 tablespoons Chinese wine or dry
  sherry
750 g (1½ lb) fillet of pork

Preparation time: 10 minutes,
  plus marinating
Cooking time: 18-20 minutes
Oven: 200°C, 400°F, Gas
  Mark 6

1. Mix together the bean curd, soy sauce, bean sauce, oil, sugar and wine. Rub the mixture on to the pork and leave to marinate for 1 hour.
2. Place the marinated pork on a wire tray in a roasting tin and place in a preheated oven to roast for 18-20 minutes.
3. Remove from the oven. Cut the pork fillet across the grain into thick slices and serve immediately on a bed of lettuce leaves.

Vegetable Fried Rice

5 tablespoons vegetable oil
1 garlic clove, crushed
3 slices root ginger, shredded
1 onion, finely chopped
1 red pepper, cored, seeded and sliced
4 dried Chinese mushrooms, soaked
  for 20 minutes, drained, stemmed
  and sliced
¼ cucumber, sliced
50 g (2 oz) peas

4 tomatoes, chopped
2 teaspoons salt
1 tablespoon winter pickle
450 g (1 lb) cooked rice
2 tablespoons soy sauce

Preparation time: 30 minutes,
  plus soaking
Cooking time: 6-7 minutes

1. Heat the oil in a wok and add the garlic and ginger. Stir-fry for 1 minute then discard. Add the vegetables, salt and winter pickle and stir-fry over medium heat for 2-3 minutes. The vegetables should still be crunchy.
2. Add the rice and mix well for 2-3 minutes until heated through.
3. Sprinkle with the soy sauce, mix well and serve.

Meat Patties with Water Chestnuts

馬
蹄
肉
餅

450 g (1 lb) minced pork
15 canned water chestnuts, chopped
3 dried Chinese mushrooms, soaked
   for 20 minutes, drained, stemmed
   and diced
2 teaspoons salt
pinch of MSG
½ teaspoon light soy sauce
pinch of freshly ground white pepper
½ teaspoon sesame oil
1 tablespoon cornflour
2 tablespoons vegetable oil
2 spring onions, finely chopped
1 garlic clove, crushed
1 shallot, finely chopped
225 g (8 oz) spinach, washed but
   not drained
1 tablespoon Chinese wine or dry
   sherry
120 ml (4 fl oz) chicken stock

**Preparation time: 15 minutes,
   plus soaking
Cooking time: 10 minutes**

1. In a bowl, mix together the pork, water chestnuts and mushrooms. Season with the salt, MSG, soy sauce, white pepper and sesame oil. Beat the mixture until thoroughly combined.
2. Divide the mixture into 24 equal portions and form into meat patties. Dust lightly with cornflour.
3. Heat the oil in a wok. Add the spring onions, garlic and shallot. Stir-fry for 30 seconds to flavour the oil, then remove and discard. Put in the meat patties and fry about 1½ minutes on either side until golden brown. Drain on paper towels then place on a warm serving dish. Pour off the oil from the wok.
4. Place the spinach in a pan and sauté quickly over heat for about 2 minutes. Drain and arrange around the meat patties.
5. Blend 1 teaspoon of the remaining cornflour with 1 tablespoon chicken stock. Reheat the wok and add the wine, remaining chicken stock and cornflour. Bring to the boil, stir well until the sauce has thickened, then pour over the meat patties. Serve hot.

Clockwise from the front: Vegetable Fried Rice, Cha Siu Roast Pork, Meat Patties with Water Chestnuts
Illustration: Calligrapher writing with a brush.

Two attractive dishes which are fun to serve and excellent for entertaining. The bird's nest is made of deep-fried grated potato. You can buy special sieves for making these 'nests' but two ordinary metal sieves will do. Menu serves 4–6.

Red and White Prawns with Green Vegetables

鴛
鴦
蝦
仁

450 g (1 lb) uncooked prawns, peeled and deveined
2 teaspoons salt
1 egg white
1 tablespoon cornflour
600 ml (1 pint) vegetable oil
225 g (8 oz) mangetout, peas or broccoli
2 spring onions, finely chopped
2 slices root ginger, finely chopped
2 tablespoons Chinese wine or dry sherry
1 tablespoon tomato purée
1 tablespoon chilli sauce

Preparation time: 10 minutes
Cooking time: 7-8 minutes

1. Mix the prawns with a pinch of salt, the egg white and the cornflour.
2. Heat 3 tablespoons of oil in a wok and add the remaining salt. Add the vegetables, stir-fry for about 1½ minutes, then remove from the wok. Place on a warmed serving dish.
3. Add the remaining oil and reheat the wok until smoking. Add the prawns and stir-fry for about 1 minute. Remove and drain on paper towels.
4. Pour off all but 1 tablespoon of the oil and reheat the wok. Add the spring onions and ginger root, followed by the prawns and wine and stir-fry for 3-4 minutes. Remove half of the prawns and arrange on top of the vegetables at one end of the dish.
5. Add the tomato purée and chilli sauce and stir to blend into the sauce. Arrange the prawns in sauce at the other end of the serving dish and serve immediately.

Chicken with Cashew Nuts in a Bird's Nest

雀
巢
腰
果
鸡
丁

350 g (12 oz) chicken breast, diced
2 tablespoons Chinese wine or dry sherry
2 tablespoons soy sauce
1 egg white
175 g (6 oz) cornflour
pinch of freshly ground white pepper
225 g (8 oz) potatoes, peeled
½ teaspoon salt
1.2 litres (2 pints) vegetable oil
1 crisp lettuce, finely shredded
1 small chilli, seeded and finely chopped
1 garlic clove, crushed
1 red pepper, cored, seeded and diced

1 green pepper, cored, seeded and diced
100 g (4 oz) canned water chestnuts, drained and diced
1 teaspoon wine vinegar
1 teaspoon sugar
1 tablespoon black bean sauce
1 teaspoon sesame oil
pinch of MSG
1 tablespoon water
225 g (8 oz) cashew nuts

Preparation time: 30 minutes, plus marinating
Cooking time: about 10 minutes

1. Place the diced chicken in a bowl with 1 tablespoon wine, 1 tablespoon soy sauce, the egg white, 1 tablespoon cornflour and white pepper. Leave to marinate for at least 20 minutes.

2. Grate the potatoes finely and rinse under cold running water. Drain and pat dry. Place in a bowl with the salt and all but 1 tablespoon of the remaining cornflour and mix well. Spoon the potato mixture into a wire sieve and spread out in a thin, even layer. Put another sieve of the same size inside the other on top of the potatoes.

3. Heat the oil in a wok to 180°C/350°F, or until a cube of bread browns in 30 seconds, then put in the 2 sieves with the potatoes trapped between. Fry gently until the potatoes are golden brown and crisp, about 4 minutes. Remove from the oil and drain on paper towels, then carefully remove the bird's nest from the sieves. Place the bird's nest on a serving dish and surround with shredded lettuce.

4. Pour off all but 4 tablespoons of the oil. Reheat the wok. When the oil begins to smoke, add the chilli and garlic, stir-fry for a few seconds then add the chicken. Stir-fry until the chicken changes colour, then remove to a warm dish.

5. Reheat the wok and add another tablespoon of oil. Add the peppers and water chestnuts. Stir-fry together for about 1-2 minutes then put on the dish with the chicken.

6. Wipe the wok clean, add 1 tablespoon of oil and reheat. Add the remaining soy sauce, wine vinegar, sugar, black bean sauce, sesame oil, MSG and the remaining teaspoon of cornflour mixed with the water. Bring to the boil, stirring continuously until it thickens. Return the chicken, peppers and water chestnuts to the wok. Toss together to reheat, then add the cashew nuts. Spoon the mixture into the bird's nest and serve immediately.

Left: Red and White Prawns with Green Vegetables
Right: Chicken with Cashew Nuts in a Bird's Nest

An assortment of Dim Sum, the teatime snacks served in tea houses in China. Many restaurants in this country serve these appetizing starters, which are pushed round on heated trolleys for the customer to choose from. You could also serve Fish Rolls (*page 88*), and Crispy Spring Rolls (*page 103*).

Crispy Wonton with Sweet and Sour Sauce

175 g (6 oz) finely minced pork
50 g (2 oz) peeled shrimps, minced
1 teaspoon salt
pinch of freshly ground white pepper
1 tablespoon soy sauce
1 packet ready-made wonton skins
600 ml (1 pint) vegetable oil
Sauce:
1 tablespoon cornflour
4 tablespoons water
1 tablespoon tomato purée
2 tablespoons wine vinegar
2 tablespoons orange juice
2 teaspoons light soy sauce
1½ tablespoons sugar
2 teaspoons vegetable oil

Preparation time: 30 minutes
Cooking time: about 7-8 minutes

1. Place the pork, minced shrimps, salt, pepper and soy sauce in a bowl and beat together until well blended. Place 1 teaspoon of stuffing in the centre of each wonton skin, gather up the corners and twist to enclose.
2. Heat the oil in a wok to 180°C/350°F, or until a cube of bread browns in 30 seconds. Add the wontons and deep-fry for 2½ minutes, then remove and drain on paper towels. Keep hot.
3. Blend the cornflour with the water, then place in a pan with the other sauce ingredients. Stir together for medium heat for 3-4 minutes, then pour into a bowl and serve with the wontons.

Steamed Siu Mai

450 g (1 lb) minced pork
6 dried Chinese mushrooms, soaked for 20 minutes, drained, stemmed and finely chopped
5 cm (2 inch) piece canned bamboo shoot, drained and finely chopped
100 g (4 oz) peeled prawns, finely chopped
2 eggs, lightly beaten
½ teaspoon salt
1 spring onion, finely chopped
pinch of MSG
pinch of freshly ground white pepper
½ teaspoon sugar
2 tablespoons vegetable oil
2 tablespoons cornflour
1 teaspoon sesame oil
100 g (4 oz) ready-made wonton skins

Preparation time: 20 minutes
Cooking time: 10 minutes

1. In a bowl, mix together the pork, mushrooms, bamboo shoot, prawns and eggs. Add the salt, spring onion, MSG, white pepper, sugar, vegetable oil, cornflour and sesame oil. Beat everything together.
2. Place about 1 teaspoon of the meat mixture in the centre of each wonton skin, then pull the edges up and twist to close tightly.
3. Place the dumplings in a steamer and cook for 10 minutes. Serve hot.

Peking Dumplings

450 g (1 lb) plain flour
175 ml (6 fl oz) boiling water
120 ml (4 fl oz) cold water, plus 1 tablespoon
450 g (1 lb) minced pork
100 g (4 oz) peeled shrimps, minced
1 tablespoon finely chopped spring onion
1 tablespoon shredded root ginger
1 tablespoon light soy sauce
1½ teaspoons salt
1 teaspoon sugar
450 g (1 lb) Chinese cabbage, finely shredded and blanched
pinch of freshly ground black pepper
pinch of MSG

Preparation time: 20 minutes
Cooking time: 20 minutes

1. Place the flour in a bowl with the boiling water. Beat well until smooth. Leave for a few minutes, then add 120 ml (4 fl oz) cold water. Knead well.
2. Mix together the pork, shrimps, onion, ginger, soy sauce, salt, sugar and remaining water. Blend well, then add the cabbage and mix into a paste.
3. Roll the dough into a long sausage shape 4 cm (1½ inch) thick. Divide into 3 cm (1¼ inch) lengths and roll flat into small pancake shapes. Place 1 tablespoon of stuffing on each pancake, then fold the pancake in half and pinch the edges together to close.
4. Steam for 20 minutes and serve.

Sauté Dumplings

鍋
貼
餃

450 g (1 lb) plain flour
175 ml (6 fl oz) boiling water
120 ml (6 fl oz) cold water
450 g (1 lb) minced pork
100 g (4 oz) peeled shrimps, minced
1 tablespoon finely chopped spring
  onion
1 tablespoon shredded root ginger
1 tablespoon light soy sauce
1½ teaspoons salt
pinch of freshly ground black pepper
pinch of MSG
1 bunch watercress, coarsely chopped
5½ tablespoons vegetable oil
Dip:
2 tablespoons wine vinegar
2 tablespoons soy sauce

Preparation time: 30 minutes
Cooking time: about 10 minutes

1. Place the flour in a bowl with the boiling water. Beat well until smooth. Leave to rest for a few minutes, then add the cold water and knead well.
2. Mix together the pork, shrimps, spring onion, ginger, soy sauce, salt, pepper and MSG. Add the chopped watercress and 1 tablespoon of the oil. Blend well together.
3. Roll the dough into a long sausage shape 4 cm (1½ inch) thick. Divide into 3 cm (1¼ inch) lengths and roll flat into small pancake shapes. Place 1 tablespoon of stuffing on each pancake, then fold the pancake in half and pinch the edges together to close.
4. Heat a wok and add 3 tablespoons of oil. Tilt the wok several times until the surface is evenly oiled. Arrange the dumplings evenly over the pan, turn the heat to high and shallow-fry

for 2-3 minutes to brown the under-side of the dumplings.
5. Add ⅔ cup of water to the wok and cover. Steam over high heat until almost all the water has evaporated. Remove the cover and pour in 1½ tablespoons of hot oil from the side. Lower the heat and cook until all the liquid has evaporated.
6. Use a fish slice to loosen the dumplings from the bottom of the wok. Place a large serving dish upside down over the wok, then invert so that the dumplings sit on the dish browned side upwards. Serve with the dip sauce mixed.

Clockwise from the front: Crispy Wonton with Sweet and Sour Sauce, Steamed Siu Mai, Peking Dumplings, Sauté Dumplings
Illustration: A travelling coppersmith.

西
部
:
四
川

Szechuan, the largest single province in China, lies in a great basin ringed with mountains. Its principal connection eastwards is through spectacular gorges cut by the Yangtse River – until recently, in fact, the Yangtse was its only means of communication with the outside world. With its fertile soil and warm, humid climate crops can be grown almost all the year round, and it has always been one of the most prosperous regions of China. Fruit and vegetables grow in abundance, as well as edible mushrooms and fungi. Spices grow in abundance here too, particularly chillis and the famous Szechuan peppercorns.

Szechuan food is noted for being hot, spicy and strongly flavoured. Chillis are used in large quantities – usually unseeded – as well as pungent flavoured vegetables such as garlic, onions and spring onions. They also enjoy the aromatic, nutty flavour of peanuts, sesame seeds, cashews, walnuts and pine nuts, which are often found incorporated into dishes; aromatic ground rice and sesame seeds are often used to coat meat which is to be deep-fried or stir-fried, while sesame paste is often the principal ingredient in sauces.

The region is also noted for its food preservation techniques, which include salting, drying, smoking and pickling, probably because the humid climate makes it difficult to keep food fresh.

Beef appears more often on the menu here than in the south – probably because oxen are used extensively for haulage. A favourite way of cooking it is by stir-frying, often until it is quite dry, giving it the characteristic dry 'chewy' texture. Steaming is also popular, and here the meat is usually first coated with ground rice, producing a rich, thick gravy.

Yunnan, in the deep south west, is even more remote than Szechuan. Being so mountainous and secluded, it developed over the years a highly distinctive cuisine of its own. The best known product of Yunnan is its ham, which many Chinese consider the best in the world. It is also noted for its game, such as rabbit and venison, and it is here that such exotic items as bear's paws, snails, armadillo, slugs and snakes can appear on the menu!

Double-Cooked Pork is one of the best-known dishes of Szechuan. Double-cooking is a technique in which the meat is first tenderized by long, slow cooking, followed by a quick crisping or stir-frying in a sauce. Menu serves 4.

Eight-Treasure Soup

600 ml (1 pint) chicken stock
50 g (2 oz) peeled prawns
50 g (2 oz) chicken breast, shredded
50 g (2 oz) pork fillet, thinly shredded
1 lettuce heart, separated into leaves
50 g (2 oz) spinach, shredded
1 cake bean curd, cut into 1 cm (½ inch) cubes
2 medium tomatoes, skinned and chopped roughly
1 tablespoon soy sauce
25 g (1 oz) Szechuan pickle, chopped
salt
good pinch freshly ground black pepper
1 egg, beaten
1 spring onion, finely chopped, to garnish

Preparation time: 20 minutes
Cooking time: 10 minutes

1. Bring the stock to the boil, put in the prawns, chicken and pork. When they start to float to the surface, add the lettuce, spinach, bean curd and tomatoes, together with the soy sauce and pickle. Cook for about 1 minute.
2. Add salt and pepper then pour in the beaten egg and stir. Garnish with finely chopped spring onion and serve immediately.

Quick-Fry Spinach in Garlic Bean Curd Cheese

3 tablespoons vegetable oil
2 garlic cloves, crushed
2 cakes bean curd cheese
1 tablespoon chilli sauce
450 g (1 lb) spinach, washed
½ teaspoon sugar
pinch of salt
pinch of MSG

Preparation time: 5 minutes
Cooking time: 3 minutes

Double-Cooked Pork

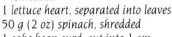

450 g (1 lb) piece of boneless pork (neck or lean belly of pork)
2 slices root ginger, chopped
1 spring onion, finely chopped
3 tablespoons vegetable oil
3 garlic cloves, thinly sliced
2 green peppers, cored, seeded and cut into 2.5 cm (1 inch) squares
2 red peppers, cored, seeded and cut into 2.5 cm (1 inch) squares
2 tablespoons sweet bean paste
1 tablespoon hot Szechuan bean paste
2 tablespoons soy sauce
2 tablespoons sugar
1 tablespoon Chinese wine or dry sherry

Preparation time: 10 minutes
Cooking time: 30 minutes

1. Boil the pork with the ginger and spring onion for 25 minutes, then drain and cool. Cut into thin slices.
2. Heat the oil in a wok and add the pork slices. Stir-fry over high heat for 2-3 minutes, then remove and drain.
3. Reheat the wok and add the garlic and peppers. Stir-fry for 1 minute, then add the sweet bean paste, hot bean paste, soy sauce, sugar and wine. Stir well then return the pork to the wok, to reheat.

1. Heat a wok and add the vegetable oil. When hot, add the garlic, bean curd cheese and chilli sauce and quick-fry for a few seconds until well mashed and evenly mixed.
2. Add the spinach to the wok together with the sugar, salt and MSG. Stir-fry for 2-3 minutes then serve.

From the left: Eight Treasure Soup, Double-Cooked Pork, Quick-Fry Spinach in Garlic Bean Curd Cheese

This menu for 4 combines an intriguing assortment of flavours. Don't be misled by the name of the chicken dish — 'Strange Flavour' Chicken is actually delicious.

Beef and Tomato Soup

100 g (4 oz) beef steak, thinly sliced
1 teaspoon salt
freshly ground black pepper
50 g (2 oz) Szechuan pickle, chopped
1 tablespoon cornflour
600 ml (1 pint) beef stock
225 g (8 oz) tomatoes, skinned and
    chopped roughly

Preparation time: 5 minutes
Cooking time: 2 minutes

1. Mix the beef with a good pinch of salt and pepper and the pickle and rub with the cornflour.
2. Bring the stock to a rolling boil, put in the beef and tomatoes, add the remaining salt and let the soup boil for 1 minute before serving.

Szechuan 'Strange Flavour' Chicken

2 teaspoons shredded root ginger
1 teaspoon Szechuan peppercorns
2 tablespoons Chinese wine or dry
    sherry
pinch of MSG
6 chicken thighs, skinned
225 g (8 oz) cashew nuts, roasted
225 g (8 oz) cucumber, diced
1 spring onion, chopped
½ teaspoon salt
2 teaspoons sugar
1 tablespoon soy sauce
1 tablespoon wine vinegar
3 tablespoons sesame paste or
    peanut butter
1 teaspoon red chilli oil
cucumber slices, to garnish

Preparation time: 15 minutes,
**   plus marinating**
Cooking time: 12 minutes

1. Mix together half the ginger, the peppercorns, wine and MSG and marinate the chicken for 30 minutes. Place in an ovenproof dish and steam for 12 minutes, then remove the bones and dice the meat.
2. Place the diced chicken, cashew nuts, cucumber, remaining ginger and spring onion in a mixing bowl.
3. Mix together the salt, sugar, soy sauce, vinegar and sesame paste in a bowl and then toss the chicken mixture in the sauce. Arrange on a serving dish and serve cold garnished with cucumber, with the chilli oil sprinkled on top.

Above, from the top: Szechuan 'Strange Flavour' Chicken, Beef and Tomato Soup. Right: Broad Beans Chungking Style, Sweet Potato Fritters
Illustration: A travelling dressmaker.

Broad Beans Chungking Style

3 tablespoons vegetable oil
450 g (1 lb) broad beans, blanched and skinned
1 tablespoon hot Szechuan bean paste
2 teaspoons salt
3 tablespoons sugar
4 spring onions, finely chopped
2 tablespoons water

Preparation time: 3 minutes
Cooking time: 17 minutes

1. Heat the oil in a wok until smoking, put in the beans and stir-fry for 2-3 minutes over medium heat.
2. Add the bean paste, salt, sugar and spring onions and stir-fry for 1-2 minutes. Put in the water and cook for another 10-15 minutes until the broad beans are soft. Serve hot or cold.

Sweet Potato Fritters

1.25 kg (2½ lb) sweet potatoes, peeled and cut into thick chips
4 tablespoons lard or cooking oil
6 tablespoons golden syrup

Preparation time: 15 minutes
Cooking time: 6 minutes

1. Put the potato chips in boiling water and cook for 3-4 minutes. Drain thoroughly.
2. Melt the lard in a wok over medium heat, add the potato chips and turn for 2-3 minutes until well coated. Drain and place in a serving bowl.
3. Heat 6 tablespoons golden syrup in a pan until melted, then pour over the chips. Turn until well coated with syrup and serve warm.

Many Szechuan dishes have a more 'chewy' texture than elsewhere in China — this is achieved by frying or stir-frying food until it is quite dry and even crusty, then tossing it in a sauce. The flavour is highly concentrated when food is cooked in this way. Multiple flavourings are also an important element, as in the beef dish, so it is quite usual to find garlic, chillis, sugar, vinegar, etc. all in one dish. Serve this meal with rice. The stuffed aubergines make ideal 'finger food' and could be served as a starter, with a dip of mixed salt and crushed Szechuan peppercorns. Menu serves 4-6.

Szechuan Hot-Fried Crispy Shredded Beef

4 eggs
½ teaspoon salt
100 g (4 oz) cornflour
450 g (1 lb) topside of beef, cut into matchstick strips
600 ml (1 pint) vegetable oil
3 medium carrots, scraped and cut into matchstick strips
2 spring onions, cut into 2.5 cm (1 inch) sections
2 chillis, shredded
3 garlic cloves, crushed
6 teaspoons sugar
2 tablespoons soy sauce
4 tablespoons wine vinegar

Preparation time: 20 minutes
Cooking time: 10 minutes

1. Mix together the eggs, salt and cornflour and toss the beef in this until well coated. Heat the oil in a wok to 180°C/350°F, or until a cube of bread browns in 30 seconds, and stir-fry the beef for 1½ minutes or until crispy. Remove and drain on paper towels.
2. Reheat the oil and deep-fry the carrots for 1½ minutes. Remove and drain on paper towels.
3. Pour off most of the oil, leaving about 1½ tablespoons in the bottom of the wok. Reheat, then add the spring onions, chillis and garlic. Stir-fry together for about 30 seconds over the heat then add the sugar, soy sauce and vinegar. Return the meat and carrots to the sauce. Toss over the heat and serve.

Deep-Fried Aubergine Cake

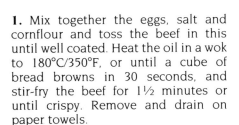

3 aubergines, cut into 2.5 cm (1 inch) thick slices
75 g (3 oz) minced pork
25 g (1 oz) dried shrimps, soaked for 20 minutes, drained and finely chopped
½ teaspoon salt
2 spring onions, finely chopped
1 tablespoon soy sauce
1 tablespoon sesame oil
1 tablespoon shredded root ginger
125 g (5 oz) plain flour
50 g (2 oz) cornflour
1 egg, beaten
2 tablespoons water
600 ml (1 pint) vegetable oil

Preparation time: 10 minutes
Cooking time: 5 minutes

1. Cut a slit in each aubergine slice, deep enough for the stuffing.
2. Mix together the minced pork, shrimps, salt, spring onion, soy sauce, sesame oil and ginger. Beat well together and stuff each aubergine slice with ½ teaspoon of filling.
3. Dust each slice with plain flour, then mix the remaining flour with the cornflour, egg and water to form a batter. Coat each slice well.
4. Heat the oil in a wok to 180°C/350°F, or until a cube of bread browns in 30 seconds, and deep-fry each slice until bright yellow. Drain well.

Bean Curd and Prawn Soup

50 g (2 oz) peeled prawns
1 egg white
600 ml (1 pint) chicken stock
50 g (2 oz) cooked ham, cut into 1 cm (½ inch) cubes
1 cake bean curd, cut into 1 cm (½ inch) cubes
50 g (2 oz) peas
1 tablespoon soy sauce
25 g (1 oz) Szechuan pickle, chopped
1 tablespoon cornflour
1 tablespoon water
salt
freshly ground black pepper

Preparation time: 10 minutes
Cooking time: 3 minutes

1. Mix the peeled prawns with the egg white.
2. Bring the stock to the boil, put in the ham, bean curd and peas. When it comes back to the boil, add the soy sauce, pickle and prawns, and let the soup boil for 15-20 seconds.
3. Blend the cornflour with the water and add to the soup, stirring constantly. Allow to thicken, then add salt and pepper to taste before serving.

Clockwise from top: Deep-Fried Aubergine Cake, Bean Curd and Prawn Soup, Szechuan Hot-Fried Crispy Shredded Beef
Illustration: Paper-making on a bamboo frame.

Smoked food is highly characteristic of Szechuan – this duck recipe is one of the best-known dishes of the region. Menu serves 6.

Szechuan Smoked Duck

1 duck, about 1.5 kg (3 lb)
2 tablespoons salt
3 teaspoons Szechuan peppercorns
½ teaspoon dried sage
1½ teaspoons ground ginger
1 teaspoon sugar
1.2 litres (2 pints) chicken stock
1 tablespoon 5-spice powder
6 spring onions, roughly chopped
6 slices root ginger, peeled
600 ml (1 pint) vegetable oil
sesame oil
Fuel for smoking:
4 tablespoons damp tea leaves
2 tablespoons brown sugar
2 tablespoons 5-spice powder
6 bay leaves
1 cup hardwood sawdust

Preparation time: 15 minutes, plus drying
Cooking time: about 55 minutes

1. Dry the duck with paper towels. Mix together three-quarters of the salt, half the Szechuan peppercorns, the sage, ginger powder and sugar. Rub the inside of the duck with this mixture, then leave in a cool draughty place to dry for 24 hours.
2. Place the duck in a large pan and cover it with water. Bring to the boil and then discard the water. Replace it with the stock, add the 5-spice powder, spring onions and ginger, and bring back to the boil. Simmer for 20 minutes, then drain.
3. Lay the fuel for smoking in the bottom of an old wok and place a wire rack on top. Place the wok over high heat and wait until it begins to smoke. Place the duck on the rack, cover the wok with foil or a lid, and smoke for 10 minutes on either side, or until the colour darkens to a golden brown.
4. Heat the oil in another wok until it is smoking. Lower the duck into the oil and deep-fry over medium heat for 10 minutes. Remove and drain.
5. Brush the duck with sesame oil and serve hot or cold.

Red Oil Dumplings

450 g (1 lb) plain flour
150 ml (¼ pint) boiling water
85 ml (3 fl oz) cold water
450 g (1 lb) minced pork
100 g (4 oz) peeled shrimps, minced
1 tablespoon chopped root ginger
1 tablespoon chopped spring onions
1½ teaspoons salt
1 tablespoon soy sauce
1 teaspoon sugar
1 tablespoon water
2 leaves Chinese cabbage, finely chopped
pinch of MSG
pinch of pepper
2 teaspoons sesame oil
Dip Sauce:
1 spring onion, finely chopped
1 garlic clove, finely chopped
2 tablespoons peanut butter
2 teaspoons soy sauce
1 teaspoon red chilli oil
2 teaspoons chicken stock

Preparation time: 40 minutes
Cooking time: 6 minutes

1. Sift the flour into a bowl. Pour on the boiling water, stirring to form a firm dough. Leave a few minutes and add the cold water. Knead to form a smooth dough.

2. In a bowl, mix together the pork, shrimps, ginger, spring onions, salt, soy sauce, sugar, water, Chinese cabbage, MSG, pepper and oil. Beat together to form a paste.

3. Form the dough into a long sausage. Divide into 5 cm (2 inch) lengths. Roll each piece into a ball and then roll flat into a small pancake. Place about 1 tablespoon of filling on each pancake and then fold the pancake over to form a half circle, enclosing the stuffing. Pinch the edges firmly to seal.

4. Place the dumplings in boiling water for 5-6 minutes. Drain on paper towels and serve hot.

5. Mix together the Dip sauce ingredients. Use either as a dip or pour over the dumplings.

Double-Cooked Pork with Black Beans

450 g (1 lb) neck or belly of pork
1 tablespoon vegetable oil
2 spring onions, finely chopped
2 slices root ginger, peeled and finely chopped
1 garlic clove, crushed
3 leaves Chinese cabbage, cut into 2.5 cm (1 inch) sections
½ teaspoon hot Szechuan bean paste
1 tablespoon yellow bean paste
1 teaspoon soy sauce
2 teaspoons sugar

1 tablespoon chicken stock
1 teaspoon salt
1 tablespoon Chinese wine or dry sherry
½ teaspoon red chilli oil

Preparation time: 10 minutes
Cooking time: 30 minutes

1. Cover the pork with water and bring to the boil. Simmer for 30 minutes and then remove, drain and allow to cool. Cut across the grain into 1 cm (½ inch) thick slices.

2. Heat the oil in a wok and add the spring onions, ginger and garlic. Stir-fry quickly together, then add the sliced pork and Chinese cabbage.

3. Mix together the hot bean paste, yellow bean paste, soy sauce, sugar, chicken stock, salt and wine and pour into the wok.

4. Toss together and bring to the boil. Arrange on a warmed serving dish and sprinkle over the chilli oil.

Quick-Fried Mangetout with Beansprouts

4 tablespoons vegetable oil
75 g (3 oz) Szechuan pickle, finely shredded
350 g (12 oz) mangetout, sliced
450 g (1 lb) beansprouts
2 teaspoons salt
3 tablespoons water
2 teaspoons sesame oil

Preparation time: 10 minutes
Cooking time: 5 minutes

1. Heat the oil in a wok. Add the pickle and mangetout. Stir-fry over high heat for 2 minutes.

2. Add the beansprouts, and sprinkle with the salt and water. Continue to stir-fry over high heat for 2 minutes. Sprinkle with sesame oil and serve.

Above left: Double-Cooked Pork with Black Beans. Above right: Quick-Fried Mangetout with Beansprouts. Left: Red Oil Dumplings. Far left: Szechuan Smoked Duck

Since Szechuan is some 1,000 miles inland, most of its fish dishes are freshwater — eel, carp, pike, perch, etc. The fish is often simply deep-fried as here, and then served in a thick, strong-tasting sauce. Menu serves 6.

Cold Mixed Kidneys

500 g (1 ¼ lb) pig's kidneys,
    skinned, halved and core removed
3 slices root ginger, peeled and thinly
    shredded
Sauce:
1 teaspoon salt
2 tablespoons Chinese wine or dry
    sherry
1 tablespoon sesame oil
2 garlic cloves, crushed
2 tablespoons chopped spring onions
2 tablespoons dark soy sauce
1½ tablespoons vegetable oil

**Preparation time: 10 minutes,
    plus marinating
Cooking time: 1-2 minutes**

1. Score the surface of the kidneys diagonally in a criss-cross pattern then cut them into thin slices. Blanch the kidney slices in boiling water. Do not over-cook: as soon as the water comes back to the boil, remove and drain under cold running water. Place them on a serving dish.
2. Sprinkle the thinly shredded ginger over the kidney slices. Mix the sauce ingredients and pour it evenly over them. Leave to marinate for at least 10-15 minutes before serving.

Szechuan Prawns

450 g (1 lb) uncooked prawns,
    peeled and deveined
1 teaspoon salt
pinch of freshly ground white pepper
1 egg white
1 tablespoon cornflour
6 tablespoons vegetable oil
2 slices root ginger, shredded
1 dried chilli, seeded and finely
    chopped
2 green peppers, cored, seeded and
    diced
1 tablespoon soy sauce
1 tablespoon chicken stock
lemon and lime slices, to garnish

**Preparation time: 10 minutes
Cooking time: 8 minutes**

1. Mix together the prawns, salt, pepper, egg white and cornflour.
2. Heat 4 tablespoons of oil in a wok until smoking, then add the prawns. Stir-fry until opaque, about 1½ minutes, then remove and drain.
3. Add the remaining oil and reheat the wok. Add the ginger and chilli, stir-fry together for about 2 seconds, then return the prawns to the wok. Add the peppers, soy sauce and stock. Toss over the heat and serve garnished with lemon and lime slices, if liked.

Fried Fish in Hot Five Willow Sauce

1 tablespoon shredded root ginger
1 tablespoon salt
600 ml (1 pint) vegetable oil
1 carp, perch or pike, about 1.25-
    1.5 kg (2½-3 lb)
3 tablespoons lard
3 spring onions, cut into 5 cm
    (2 inch) sections
1 small green pepper, cored, seeded
    and cut into strips
1 small red pepper, cored, seeded and
    cut into strips
2 chillis, seeded and shredded
2 rashers bacon, shredded
2 tablespoons winter pickle
3 tablespoons chicken stock
2 teaspoons sugar
2 tablespoons dry sherry
3½ tablespoons soy sauce

1 tablespoon yellow bean paste
1 ½ tablespoons sweet bean paste
2 tablespoons cornflour
3 tablespoons water

Preparation time: 20 minutes
Cooking time: about 20 minutes

1. Mix half the ginger with the salt and 1 tablespoon oil. Rub the fish inside and out with this mixture.
2. Heat the oil in a wok until smoking and deep-fry the fish for 6 minutes. Remove and drain.
3. Heat the lard in another wok. Add all the vegetables for the sauce as well as the bacon and pickle and stir-fry over a high heat for 2 minutes. Add the stock, sugar, sherry, soy sauce, bean paste and sweet bean paste. Blend the cornflour with the water and stir into the sauce. Lower the fish into the sauce. Cook, basting with the liquid, for 1½ minutes. Turn the fish and cook for another 2½ minutes. Reduce the heat and cook slowly for 5 more minutes then serve.

Cold or Hot-Tossed Noodles

6 tablespoons vegetable oil
225 g (8 oz) beansprouts
225 g (8 oz) lean pork, cut into matchstrip strips
½ teaspoon salt
1 tablespoon soy sauce
1 tablespoon chilli sauce
½ teaspoon sugar
75 g (3 oz) Szechuan pickle, shredded
3 spring onions, shredded
3 tablespoons water
750 g (1½ lb) fresh egg noodles, or 450 g (1 lb) dried noodles

Preparation time: 10 minutes
Cooking time: 10-15 minutes

1. Heat 2 tablespoons of the oil in a wok and add the beansprouts. Stir-fry quickly for 1 minute; then remove and drain on paper towels.

2. Add the remaining oil to the wok and reheat. Add the pork, salt, soy sauce, chilli sauce, sugar, pickle and spring onions. Stir-fry together for 4 minutes, then add the water and return the beansprouts to the wok. Stir-fry for another 2 minutes.
3. Plunge the noodles into a large pan of boiling water and cook until the noodles are soft but still firm to bite — about 3 minutes for fresh noodles and 7-8 minutes for dried ones. Drain and toss with two-thirds of the pork and beansprout mixture. Arrange on a large serving dish and pour the rest of the sauce on top. Serve hot or cold.

Above, from the left: Fried Fish in Hot Five Willow Sauce, Cold or Hot-Tossed Noodles.
Left, from the top: Cold Mixed Kidneys, Szechuan Prawns

These oxtail noodles make a wonderfully hearty and satisfying dish with a dark, shiny sauce. The cold, spicy chicken dish is often served at banquets in China; it also makes a particularly good lunch or picnic dish. The sauce, with its unique hot, nutty taste, gives the chicken an exotic flavour. For those who don't like a hot peppery taste, the chilli oil can be omitted. Menu serves 6.

Szechuan Dan Dan Noodles

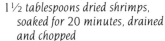

450 g (1 lb) rice stick noodles
3 tablespoons vegetable oil
1½ tablespoons dried shrimps, soaked for 20 minutes, drained and chopped
6 dried Chinese mushrooms, soaked for 20 minutes, drained, stemmed and shredded
50 g (2 oz) Szechuan pickle, chopped
2 garlic cloves, crushed
3 teaspoons minced root ginger
225 g (8 oz) minced pork
1½ tablespoons soy sauce
1 tablespoon red chilli oil or chilli sauce
2 spring onions, finely chopped
600 ml (1 pint) chicken stock
salt
freshly ground black pepper

Preparation time: 15 minutes
Cooking time: 10 minutes

1. Blanch the noodles in boiling water for 2 minutes, then drain and rinse. Keep warm.
2. Heat the oil in a wok and add the shrimps, mushrooms, pickle, garlic and ginger. Stir-fry for 30 seconds and then add the minced pork.
3. Mix the pork with other ingredients over high heat for 4 minutes. Mix the soy sauce, red chilli oil, spring onions and 150 ml (¼ pint) of the stock together and pour into the wok. Season with salt and pepper.
4. Simmer for 5 minutes, then pour in the remaining stock and bring to the boil. Divide the noodles among the serving bowls and pour on some sauce.

Chicken with Cold-Tossed Beansprouts

1 teaspoon wine vinegar
2 teaspoons sesame oil
1½ teaspoons sugar
pinch of MSG
225 g (8 oz) beansprouts, blanched in boiling water and refreshed
2 cooked chicken breasts, cut into matchstick shreds
1½ tablespoons sesame paste or peanut butter
1 tablespoon soy sauce
1 teaspoon Worcestershire sauce
1 spring onion, finely chopped
1 slice root ginger, peeled and finely chopped
1 garlic clove, crushed
1 tablespoon red chilli oil

Preparation time: 8 minutes

1. Mix together the vinegar, 1 teaspoon sesame oil, ½ teaspoon sugar and MSG. Toss the beansprouts in this mixture. Place on a serving dish and arrange the chicken meat on top.
2. In a bowl mix together the sesame paste, soy sauce, remaining sugar, remaining sesame oil, Worcestershire sauce, spring onion, ginger and garlic. Spoon this over the chicken and then sprinkle on the red chilli oil. Serve this dish cold.

Oxtail Noodles with Parsley, Coriander and Spring Onion

牛
尾
麵

1.8 kg (4 lb) oxtail, cut up
450 g (1 lb) rice stick noodles
600 ml (1 pint) beef stock
1 chicken stock cube
4 tablespoons soy sauce
freshly ground black pepper
3 tablespoons hoisin sauce
2 tablespoons yellow bean paste
1 tablespoon sugar
6 tablespoons dry sherry
5 spring onions, finely chopped
1 1/2 tablespoons cornflour
5 tablespoons water
4 tablespoons chopped parsley
3 tablespoons chopped coriander
    leaves

Preparation time: 15 minutes
Cooking time: about 4 hours
**Oven: 180°C, 350°F, Gas
    Mark 4**

1. Parboil the oxtail in boiling water for 5-6 minutes and drain. Cook the noodles in boiling water for 5 minutes then drain.
2. Heat the stock in a casserole. Add the crumbled stock cube, soy sauce, pepper (to taste), hoisin sauce, yellow bean paste, sugar and half the sherry. Bring to the boil and add the oxtail. Stir until the oxtail is well coated with sauce. Cover and cook in a preheated oven for 3½ hours, stirring every half hour and adding more stock when necessary.
3. Place the drained noodles in a wok. Sprinkle evenly with the chopped spring onion. Pour the gravy from the casserole over the noodles and spring onion. Turn over medium heat for 3 minutes, until the noodles are heated through.

4. Pour the noodles into a large serving dish. Sprinkle the remainder of the sherry over the oxtail in the casserole. Blend the cornflour and water and stir into the casserole. Turn the oxtail over a few times, until a glossy sauce has formed.
5. Arrange the oxtail on top of the noodles in the serving dish, spoon the remaining sauce over and sprinkle with chopped parsley and coriander.

Clockwise from top: Szechuan Dan Dan Noodles, Oxtail Noodles with Parsley, Coriander and Spring Onion, Chicken with Cold-Tossed Beansprouts
Illustration: A ropemaker.

Buddhist's Delight is so-called because it is a favourite vegetarian dish, often served in temples and monasteries, but also considered good enough for a banquet. The dish, which usually has 10 different ingredients, can be eaten as a whole meal, with only rice and soup as an accompaniment. Serve the spicy, savoury frogs' legs as a starter. Menu serves 6.

Buddhist's Delight

300 ml (½ pint) vegetable oil
1 cake bean curd, cut into 1 cm (½ inch) cubes
50 g (2 oz) hair seaweed, soaked for 20 minutes, and drained
3 tablespoons pine nuts
2-3 golden needles, soaked for 30 minutes, and drained
6 dried Chinese mushrooms, soaked for 20 minutes, drained, stemmed and sliced
6 canned water chestnuts, sliced
150 g (6 oz) Chinese cabbage, cut into 4 cm (1½ inch) chunks
2 carrots, scraped and sliced
50 g (2 oz) mangetout
300 ml (½ pint) chicken stock
1 teaspoon salt
1½ tablespoons soy sauce
½ teaspoon MSG
1½ tablespoons chilli sauce
1 teaspoon sesame oil

1 tablespoon cornflour
3 tablespoons water

Preparation time: 20 minutes, plus soaking
Cooking time: 30 minutes

1. Heat the oil in a wok until it is smoking. Add the bean curd and deep-fry for 2 minutes. Remove and drain on paper towels.
2. Place the seaweed, pine nuts, golden needles, mushrooms, chestnuts, cabbage, carrots, mangetout, stock, salt, soy sauce, MSG and chilli sauce in a saucepan. Bring to the boil, lower the heat and simmer for 25 minutes.
3. Add the sesame oil, bean curd, and the cornflour blended with the water. Bring to the boil and simmer for another 2 minutes. Serve hot.

Quick-Braised Frogs' Legs

750 g-1 kg (1½-2 lb) frogs' legs, disjointed
2 tablespoons soy sauce
3 slices root ginger, peeled and shredded
2 tablespoons cornflour
300 ml (½ pint) vegetable oil
1 green pepper, cored, seeded and thinly sliced
1 red pepper, cored, seeded and thinly sliced
1 onion, thinly sliced
1½ tablespoons hot Szechuan bean paste
150 ml (¼ pint) chicken stock
2 tablespoons Chinese wine or dry sherry
1 tablespoon sugar
1 teaspoon chilli sauce
1 tablespoon sesame oil

Preparation time: 20 minutes, plus marinating
Cooking time: about 15 minutes

1. Rub the frogs' legs with the soy sauce and ginger and leave to marinate for 30 minutes. Sprinkle with cornflour, turn until well coated and leave for another 30 minutes to dry.
2. Heat the oil in a wok. Divide the frogs' legs into 2 batches, and stir-fry each batch over high heat for 2½ minutes. Drain on paper towels.
3. Pour off all but 1 tablespoon of the oil. Reheat the wok and add the peppers and onion. Stir-fry over high heat for 1½ minutes then return the frogs' legs to the pan and stir together for 1½ minutes.
4. Add the bean paste, stock, sherry, sugar and chilli sauce. Stir well, reduce heat and allow contents to simmer for 4-5 minutes. Sprinkle with the sesame oil and serve.

Long-Cooked Lamb with Tangerine Peel

1 tablespoon vegetable oil
1 tablespoon shredded root ginger
2 garlic cloves, crushed
4 spring onions, chopped
900 ml (1½ pints) chicken stock
1 tablespoon soy sauce
1 teaspoon salt
1 teaspoon Szechuan peppercorns
25 g (1 oz) dried tangerine peel, soaked for 20 minutes and drained
1 leg of lamb, about 1 kg (2 lb), boned and diced
1 tablespoon cornflour
2 tablespoons water

Preparation time: 10 minutes
Cooking time: 50 minutes

1. Heat the oil in a wok and add the ginger, garlic and half of the spring onions. Stir-fry for a few seconds, then add the chicken stock, soy sauce, salt, Szechuan peppercorns, tangerine peel and meat. Bring to the boil, cover and simmer for 45 minutes.
2. Blend the cornflour and water and stir into the wok. Bring back to the boil, stirring. Serve garnished with lettuce and remaining spring onions.

Clockwise from top: Long-Cooked Lamb with Tangerine Peel, Quick-Braised Frogs' Legs, Buddhist's Delight
Illustration: Chinese embroiderer.

Tung Po, who is said to have invented this dish, was a Chinese poet of the Song dynasty. Serve the stuffed mushrooms as a starter. Select carefully so that they are an even size and shape. Menu serves 4-6.

Long-Braised Tung Po Pork

1 kg (2 lb) belly of pork, cut into 4
   pieces
600 ml (1 pint) vegetable oil
1½ tablespoons dark soy sauce
4 tablespoons light soy sauce
300 ml (½ pint) beef stock
3 slices root ginger, peeled
1½ tablespoons sugar
3 pieces star anise

Preparation time: 10 minutes
Cooking time: 2 hours, 10
  minutes
Oven: 180°C/350°F, Gas
  Mark 4

---

1. Put the pork pieces in a pan of water and bring to the boil. Simmer for 5 minutes then drain and cool.
2. Heat the oil in a wok to 180°C/350°F, or until a cube of bread browns in 30 seconds. Rub the pork all over with the dark soy sauce, then deep-fry for 3 minutes. Remove from the oil and drain on paper towels.
3. Place the pork skin side down in a casserole and pour over the light soy sauce and stock. Add the ginger, sugar and star anise. Bring to the boil, then place in a preheated oven for about 2 hours, covered.
4. To serve, place 3 pieces of the pork in a bowl and lay the 4th across the others. Pour over the gravy from the casserole and serve hot.

Shredded Chicken in Mustard Sauce

½ teaspoon salt
2 egg whites
1 tablespoon cornflour
2 chicken breasts, shredded
150 ml (¼ pint) vegetable oil
coriander leaves, to garnish
Sauce:
2 tablespoons mustard powder
1 tablespoon light soy sauce
1 tablespoon wine vinegar
2 teaspoons sesame oil

Preparation time: 10 minutes, plus standing
Cooking time: 5 minutes

1. Mix the mustard powder with cold water to form a thin paste, and let it stand for about 30 minutes.
2. Mix the salt, egg whites and cornflour and toss the chicken in this.
3. Heat the oil in a wok and stir in the chicken over medium heat. Separate the chicken shreds with chopsticks or a fork. As soon as their colour changes to pale white, scoop out with a perforated spoon and drain on paper towels.
4. Place the shredded chicken on a serving dish. Mix the sauce well and pour it evenly over the chicken. Garnish with coriander leaves.

Braised Stuffed Mushrooms

2 eggs
2 tablespoons cornflour
15 large dried Chinese mushrooms, soaked for 20 minutes, drained and stemmed
225 g (8 oz) chicken breast, minced
50 g (2 oz) pork, minced
1 teaspoon salt
2 tablespoons vegetable oil
3 tablespoons lard
Sauce:
1 tablespoon chicken fat
2 slices root ginger, peeled and minced
3 tablespoons chicken stock
2 tablespoons chopped spring onions
2 tablespoons soy sauce
1 tablespoon hoisin sauce
2 tablespoons Chinese wine or dry sherry
2-3 tablespoons chopped ham
1 tablespoon cornflour
3 tablespoons water
1 teaspoon sesame oil

Preparation time: 30 minutes, plus soaking
Cooking time: about 10 minutes

1. Beat the eggs with the cornflour. Use half the mixture to coat the inside of the mushroom caps. Mix together the chicken, pork, salt and the remaining egg and cornflour. Divide the mixture into 15 portions and roll each one into a small ball. Press each stuffing ball inside a mushroom cap, pressing it down flat. Brush with oil.
2. Heat the lard and remaining oil in a large, flat frying pan. Carefully place the mushrooms in the pan, stuffing side down, and sauté over medium heat for 3 minutes. Turn the mushrooms and again sauté over low heat for 5 minutes.
3. Heat the chicken fat in a wok, then add the ginger, stock, spring onion, soy sauce, hoisin sauce, wine and ham. Stir over high heat for 1 minute. Blend the cornflour with the water and stir into the wok until the sauce thickens. Sprinkle with sesame oil.
4. Transfer the mushrooms to a heated serving dish. Pour the sauce over the mushrooms or serve separately.

From the left: Long-Braised Tung Po Pork, Shredded Chicken in Mustard Sauce, Braised Stuffed Mushrooms

An ideal party menu — served with rice or noodles it would serve 6-8 people. Pickles are often served as an accompaniment to rich meat or fish dishes.

Dry-Fried Shredded Eel

4 tablespoons vegetable oil
750 g (1½ lb) eel, cut into 6 cm (2½ inch) sections, then each section cut into strips, off the bone
5 slices root ginger, peeled and shredded
1 teaspoon salt
2 tablespoons Chinese wine or dry sherry
4 sticks celery, cut into strips
3 young leeks, cut into rings
1 tablespoon salted black beans, soaked and drained
1 tablespoon hot Szechuan bean paste
1½ tablespoons soy sauce
1½ tablespoons wine vinegar
2 tablespoons freshly chopped coriander leaves

Preparation time: 45 minutes
Cooking time: 8 minutes

1. Heat the oil in a wok. Add the eel and ginger and stir-fry for 3 minutes over medium heat, spreading the strips over the surface of the wok. Sprinkle with the salt and wine.
2. Add the celery, leeks, black beans, bean paste, and soy sauce. Stir well together for 2 minutes then cook over low heat for another 3 minutes.
3. To serve, turn onto a heated serving dish. Sprinkle with the vinegar and freshly chopped coriander.

Szechuan Bang-Bang Chicken

1 chicken, about 1.5 kg (3 lb)
1 cucumber, cut into matchstick strips
Sauce:
4 tablespoons peanut butter
2 teaspoons sesame oil
½ teaspoon sugar
pinch of salt
2 teaspoons chicken stock

½ teaspoon red chilli oil

Preparation time: 15 minutes
Cooking time: 30 minutes

1. Place the chicken in a large pan and cover with water. Bring to the boil and simmer for 30 minutes. Remove the chicken, allow to cool and take the meat off the bone. Cut into matchstick strips.
2. Arrange the cucumber on a serving dish and put the chicken on top.
3. Mix together the peanut butter, sesame oil, sugar, salt and stock and spoon over the chicken. Sprinkle on the red chilli oil and serve cold.

Soy-Braised Beef with Carrots

紅燒牛肉

1 ½ tablespoons vegetable oil
750 g (1 ½ lb) braising beef, cut into 2.5 cm (1 inch) cubes
3 slices root ginger, peeled
4 garlic cloves, crushed
½ teaspoon salt
1 tablespoon sugar
2 teaspoons crushed Szechuan peppercorns
2 dried chillis, finely chopped
4 tablespoons soy sauce
300 ml (½ pint) water
450 g (1 lb) carrots, scraped and cut into 1 cm (½ inch) thick slices on the slant

Preparation time: 10 minutes
Cooking time: 1 ½ hours

1. Heat the oil in a heavy casserole and add the beef. Stir to seal the meat then add the ginger, garlic, salt, sugar, peppercorns, chillis, soy sauce and water. Bring to the boil, then cover and simmer for 30 minutes.
2. Add the carrots and continue to simmer for another hour, or until the meat and carrots are tender.

Crunchy Pickled Cucumber or Cabbage

甜酸黃瓜

4 teaspoons salt
4 dried chillis, seeded and shredded
3 tablespoons gin
2 medium cucumbers or 1 large hard white cabbage, thinly sliced
600 ml (1 pint) malt vinegar

Preparation time: 10 minutes, plus marinating

1. Sprinkle the salt, chillis and gin over the cucumber. Leave to season for 2 hours.
2. Place the mixture in a jar and pour in the vinegar. Let it stand for 3 days turning or shaking once a day.

Left, top: Dry-Fried Shredded Eel. Left, bottom: Szechuan Bang-Bang Chicken. Right, top: Soy-Braised Beef with Carrots. Right, bottom: Crunchy Pickled Cucumber

Ants on the Trees is so-called because the specks of cooked meat resemble ants dotted over the noodles which symbolize tree branches. Serve the Crispy Duck in the same way as Peking Duck (page 47). Serves 4.

Crispy Rice with Chilli Prawns

锅
巴
虾
仁

50 g (2 oz) cornflour
1 egg white
2 tablespoons Chinese wine or dry sherry
½ teaspoon freshly ground white pepper
225 g (8 oz) uncooked prawns, peeled and deveined
600 ml (1 pint) vegetable oil
2 chillis, finely chopped
2 slices root ginger, peeled and finely chopped
2 spring onions, finely chopped
250 ml (8 fl oz) chicken stock
25 g (1 oz) canned bamboo shoots, drained and finely sliced
25 g (1 oz) frozen peas, thawed
25 g (1 oz) cooked ham, finely shredded
1 tablespoon tomato ketchup
2 teaspoons salt
1 tablespoon water
225 g (8 oz) crispy rice (page 32)

Preparation time: 10 minutes
Cooking time: 8 minutes

1. Mix the cornflour (reserving 2 tablespoons), egg white, wine and white pepper. Toss the prawns in the mixture until thoroughly coated.
2. Heat the oil in a wok to 180°C/ 350°F, or until a cube of bread browns in 30 seconds, then add the prawns. Stir-fry quickly for about 1 minute or until the prawns change colour. Drain on paper towels and keep warm.
3. Heat 1 tablespoon of oil in another wok or saucepan. Add the chilli, ginger and spring onions. Stir together then put in the chicken stock, bamboo shoots, peas, ham, tomato ketchup, salt and the prawns.
4. Blend the remaining cornflour with 1 tablespoon of water and stir into the mixture to thicken the sauce.
5. Reheat the wok with the oil until smoking and add the rice (it should be quite dry). This should immediately puff up and rise to the top. Remove from the oil and drain on paper towels. Place the rice in a deep bowl and pour over the prawns and sauce. Serve immediately.

Aromatic Crispy Duck

脆
皮
鸭

1 duck, about 1.5 kg (3½ lb)
1.2 litres (2 pints) chicken stock
8 tablespoons sugar
4 slices root ginger, peeled
8 tablespoons soy sauce
3 teaspoons salt
3 tablespoons dry sherry
6 pieces star anise
1 tablespoon Szechuan peppercorns
1.2 litres (2 pints) oil

Preparation time: 10 minutes
Cooking time: 3 hours 10 minutes

1. Cut the duck in half down the breastbone and backbone. Heat the rest of the ingredients, except the oil, in a large pan. Place the 2 duck halves in the pan and simmer for 3 hours.
2. Remove the duck from the pan, drain and cool.
3. When ready to serve, heat the oil in a wok to 180°C/350°F, or until a cube of bread browns in 30 seconds, and deep-fry the duck until golden brown and crisp. Drain on paper towels and shred at the table. Serve with pancakes, shredded cucumber, shredded spring onions and duck sauce (see page 47).

Ma Po Tou Fu

麻婆豆腐

3 tablespoons vegetable oil
225 g (8 oz) minced beef
1 teaspoon salt
2 tablespoons black beans, soaked, drained and crushed
4 chillis, seeded and shredded
3 spring onions, finely chopped
3 garlic cloves, crushed
4 dried Chinese mushrooms, soaked for 20 minutes, drained, stemmed and chopped
2 tablespoons winter pickle
100 ml (3½ fl oz) chicken stock
3 cakes bean curd, simmered in water for 3 minutes, drained and cut into 2.5 cm (1 inch) cubes
100 g (4 oz) frozen peas, thawed
1 tablespoon cornflour
1½ tablespoons soy sauce
½ teaspoon freshly ground black pepper

Preparation time: 20 minutes, plus soaking
Cooking time: 15 minutes

1. Heat the oil in a wok and add the beef, salt and black beans. Mix together over heat for 3-4 minutes, then add the chillis, spring onions, garlic, mushrooms and pickle.
2. Stir-fry for another 2 minutes. Add half the stock, the bean curd and peas. Simmer for 5 minutes.
3. Blend the remaining stock with the cornflour and soy sauce. Stir into the wok to thicken the sauce. Bring to the boil and serve with a sprinkling of freshly ground pepper.

Ants on the Trees

蟻蟻上樹

225 g (8 oz) minced pork
1 tablespoon dark soy sauce
1 tablespoon Chinese wine or dry sherry
1 teaspoon cornflour
3 tablespoons vegetable oil
2 spring onions, finely chopped
4 teaspoons hot Szechuan bean sauce
1 teaspoon sugar
75 g (3 oz) cellophane noodles, soaked for 20 minutes, drained and cut into 10 cm (4 inch) lengths
150 ml (¼ pint) chicken stock

Preparation time: 20 minutes, plus soaking
Cooking time: 8-10 minutes

1. Mix together the minced pork, soy sauce, wine and cornflour.
2. Heat the oil in a wok. Add the spring onions and pork and stir-fry until the meat separates. Add the bean sauce and sugar and stir well. Add the cellophane noodles, and stir to blend with the meat.
3. Pour in the chicken stock and bring to a boil. Cover and cook for about 5 minutes until the stock is absorbed. Serve hot.

Left: Crispy Rice with Chilli Prawns, Aromatic Crispy Duck
Below, from the top: Ma Po Tou Fu, Ants on the Trees
Illustration: Shaping a porcelain bowl on a potter's wheel.

Aubergines are a very popular vegetable, found in markets all over China. This Szechuan version is full of wonderful flavours. The tender-cooked aubergine chips are served with a shiny, dark brown sauce. Menu serves 4-6.

Szechuan Hot Chilli Pork

2 eggs
100 g (4 oz) cornflour
450 g (1 lb) lean pork, cut into thin slices
1.2 litres (2 pints) vegetable oil
2 carrots, scraped and cut into rings
2 garlic cloves, crushed
2 chillis, finely chopped
2 spring onions, finely chopped
2 tablespoons wine vinegar
1 tablespoon soy sauce
1½ teaspoons salt
4 tablespoons sugar
1 teaspoon sesame oil

Preparation time: 10 minutes
Cooking time: 8 minutes

1. Mix together the eggs and corn-flour and toss the meat in this mixture until well coated.
2. Heat the oil in a wok until medium hot, add the meat and cook for 2 minutes. Put in the carrots and continue to cook for another 3 minutes. Remove the meat and carrots and drain on paper towels.
3. Pour off the oil, leaving about 1 tablespoon in the bottom of the wok. Reheat the wok and put in the garlic, chillis, spring onions, vinegar, soy sauce, salt and sugar. Stir-fry quickly, then return the meat and carrots. Sprinkle on the sesame oil and serve.

Aubergines in Garlic Sauce

600 ml (1 pint) vegetable oil
450 g (1 lb) aubergines, cut into chips
2 spring onions, finely chopped
1 slice root ginger, peeled and finely chopped
1 garlic clove, crushed
100 g (4 oz) pork fillet, shredded into matchstick strips
1 tablespoon soy sauce
1 tablespoon dry sherry
2 tablespoons chilli paste
2 tablespoons cornflour
1 tablespoon water

Preparation time: 30 minutes
Cooking time: 8-10 minutes

1. Heat the oil in a wok to 180°C/350°F, or until a cube of bread browns in 30 seconds. Deep-fry the aubergine chips for 3-4 minutes then remove

Crispy Chicken

脆皮鸡

1 chicken, about 1.5 kg (3½ lb)
2½ teaspoons salt
3 slices root ginger, peeled and shredded
2 dried chillis, shredded
2 tablespoons chopped coriander leaves
2 tablespoons soy sauce
pinch of 5-spice powder
2 tablespoons Chinese wine or dry sherry
1.2 litres (2 pints) vegetable oil

Preparation time: 15 minutes, plus seasoning overnight and marinating
Cooking time: 1 hour 40 minutes
Oven: 190°C/375°F, Gas Mark 5

and drain on paper towels.
2. Pour off the oil, leaving 1 tablespoon in the bottom of the wok and reheat. Quickly stir-fry the spring onions, ginger and garlic, followed by the pork. Add the soy sauce, sherry and chilli paste and blend well.
3. Add the aubergine chips to the wok and stir together for 1-2 minutes. Blend the cornflour with the water and stir into the wok until the sauce thickens.

1. Rub the chicken with the salt inside and out and leave to season overnight.
2. Mix together the ginger, chillis, coriander leaves, soy sauce, 5 spice powder and wine. Rub the chicken with this mixture, leave for 1 hour to marinate then rub the spice mixture over the chicken again.
3. Place the chicken in a roasting tin and roast in a preheated oven for 1½ hours. Drain on paper towels then place in a wire basket.
4. Heat the oil in a wok to 180°C/350°F, or until a cube of bread browns in 30 seconds. Lower the chicken into the oil and deep-fry for 6 minutes, or until the skin is crispy. Remove and drain on paper towels.
5. Chop the chicken through the bone into 24 pieces and arrange on a serving dish. Serve hot or cold.

From the left: Szechuan Hot Chilli Pork, Aubergines in Garlic Sauce, Crispy Chicken

Steaming, which is the easiest of all the Chinese cooking techniques, is the favourite form of slow cooking in Szechuan. The meat and other ingredients are packed in layers into a heatproof bowl and given a long, slow steaming. When ready, the steamed puddings (most Chinese puddings are savoury) are often turned out on to a heated serving dish. To conserve fuel, the Chinese will often prepare a whole series of dishes to be steamed at the same time, in several layers of basket steamers. Menu serves 4.

Prawns with Chillis

2 egg whites
75 g (3 oz) cornflour, plus 1
    tablespoon
2 teaspoons salt
1 tablespoon Chinese wine or dry
    sherry
450 g (1 lb) uncooked prawns,
    peeled and deveined
300 ml (½ pint) vegetable oil
2 teaspoons tomato ketchup
pinch of freshly ground white pepper
1 teaspoon sugar
2 spring onions, finely chopped
2 slices root ginger, peeled and
    shredded
2 dried chillis, finely chopped
1 tablespoon chicken stock
1 teaspoon sesame oil
1 teaspoon red chilli oil

Preparation time: 20 minutes
Cooking time: 3-4 minutes

1. Mix together the egg whites, 75 g (3 oz) cornflour, 1 teaspoon salt and the Chinese wine. Toss the prawns in this mixture.
2. Heat the oil in a wok to 180°C/ 350°F or until a cube of bread browns in 30 seconds. Add the prawns and stir-fry for about 2 minutes. Remove the prawns and drain on paper towels.
3. Pour off most of the oil, leaving about 1 tablespoon to coat the bottom of the wok. Reheat the wok and add the tomato ketchup, white pepper, remaining salt and sugar. Return the prawns to the wok along with the finely chopped spring onions, ginger and chopped chillis. Stir-fry for 1 minute.
4. Blend the remaining cornflour with the chicken stock and stir into the wok to thicken the sauce. Pour onto a plate and sprinkle over the sesame oil and red chilli oil.

Yam and Pork Steamed Pudding

1½ tablespoons lard or vegetable oil
450 g (1 lb) minced pork
50 g (2 oz) Szechuan pickle, chopped
1 tablespoon hot Szechuan bean
    paste
1½ tablespoons hoisin sauce
½ tablespoon soy sauce
1 teaspoon salt
2 onions, finely chopped
4 garlic cloves, finely chopped
750 g (1½ lb) yams, peeled and
    thinly sliced
3 tablespoons chopped coriander
    leaves

Preparation time: 20 minutes
Cooking time: 2½ hours

1. Grease a heatproof bowl with the lard or vegetable oil. Mix together the pork, pickle, bean paste, sauces, salt, onion and garlic. Beginning with the yams, lay alternate layers of the yam and the pork mixture in the bowl, finishing with an overlapping layer of yam slices.
2. Cover the bowl with foil and steam over medium heat for 2½ hours. To serve, uncover the bowl and sprinkle with chopped fresh coriander. The pudding could also be turned out of the bowl on to a heated serving dish and then sprinkled with coriander.

Crab Meat with Green Cabbage

時
菜
扒
蟹
肉

225 g (8 oz) cabbage, roughly
  chopped
6 tablespoons vegetable oil
450 ml (¾ pint) chicken stock
1½ teaspoons salt
2 spring onions, finely chopped
2 slices root ginger, peeled and finely
  chopped
2 dried chillis, finely chopped
225 g (8 oz) crab meat
2 tablespoons Chinese wine or dry
  sherry
1½ tablespoons cornflour
2 tablespoons water
1 egg white

Preparation time: 10 minutes
Cooking time: 5 minutes

1. Blanch the cabbage in boiling water for 1 minute, then drain and refresh in cold water. Drain well.
2. Heat 2 tablespoons of the oil in a wok and add the cabbage. Stir-fry for about 1 minute then add 200 ml (7 fl oz) stock and ½ teaspoon salt. Cook together for 1 minute then remove to a warm plate.
3. Heat another 3 tablespoons of the oil in the wok, add the spring onions, ginger and chillis and stir-fry for a few seconds. Add the crab meat and wine, then the remaining stock, salt and cornflour blended with the water. Bring to the boil, stirring, then add the egg white. Stir until blended.
4. Pour the crab meat mixture on top of the cabbage. Heat the final tablespoon of oil until smoking, pour over the top and serve.

From the top: Crab Meat with Green Cabbage, Prawns with Chillis, Yam and Pork Steamed Pudding

These hot, spicy dishes are best served with plain rice or noodles. The use of peanut butter in the chicken sauce gives it a nutty, aromatic flavour. Menu serves 4.

Carp with Hot Bean Paste

1 carp or sea bass, about 1 kg
   (2¼ lb)
1 tablespoon dark soy sauce
600 ml (1 pint) vegetable oil
2 spring onions, finely chopped
2 slices root ginger, peeled and finely
   chopped
1 garlic clove, crushed
1 tablespoon hot Szechuan bean
   paste
1 tablespoon Chinese wine or dry
   sherry

1 teaspoon sugar
2 teaspoons salt
1 teaspoon freshly ground white
   pepper
1 tablespoon wine vinegar
300 ml (½ pint) chicken stock
1 tablespoon cornflour
1 tablespoon water

Preparation time: 10 minutes
Cooking time: 20 minutes

1. Make 3-4 diagonal cuts on both sides of the fish, then rub with soy sauce.
2. Heat the oil in a wok to 180°/350°F or until a cube of bread browns in 30 seconds, and deep-fry the fish until golden brown. Remove and drain on paper towels.
3. Pour off most of the oil, leaving about 1 tablespoon in the bottom of the wok. Reheat and add the spring onions, ginger, garlic, hot bean paste, wine, sugar, salt, white pepper, vinegar and chicken stock. Bring to the boil, put in the fish and simmer for about 10 minutes.
4. Remove the fish to a warmed serving dish. Blend the cornflour and water and stir into the wok to thicken the sauce. Pour over the fish and serve immediately.

Hot-Tossed Shredded Chicken in Red Oil

1 chicken, about 1.5 kg (3½ lb)
3 teaspoons salt
3 slices root ginger, peeled
1 medium onion, peeled and sliced
1 medium cucumber, shredded into
   matchsticks
Sauce:
1½ tablespoons chilli sauce
1 tablespoon finely chopped garlic
2 slices root ginger, peeled and finely
   chopped
1 tablespoon peanut butter
1 spring onion, finely chopped
3 tablespoons chicken stock
pinch of MSG
2 teaspoons sesame oil

Preparation time: 15 minutes
Cooking time: 30 minutes

1. Cover the chicken with water, and add the salt, ginger and onion. Bring to the boil and simmer for 30 minutes. Then remove, drain and cool. Shred the meat finely.
2. Arrange the cucumber shreds on a plate and place the chicken shreds on top.
3. Mix together all the ingredients for the sauce and pour over the chicken. Serve cold.

Yu-Hsiang Pork Ribbons Quick-Fried with Shredded Vegetables

4 tablespoons vegetable oil
2 dried chillis, finely chopped
50 g (2 oz) Szechuan pickle, finely
   chopped
350 g (12 oz) lean pork, finely
   shredded
3 slices root ginger, peeled and finely
   chopped
225 g (8 oz) mangetout
225 g (8 oz) Chinese cabbage,
   shredded
1 red pepper, cored, seeded and
   shredded
2 medium carrots, scraped and
   sliced into matchsticks
75 g (3 oz) beanshoots
2 garlic cloves, crushed
1 teaspoon salt
4 tablespoons chicken stock
2½ tablespoons soy sauce
1½ tablespoons hoisin sauce
1 tablespoon red chilli oil
1½ tablespoons wine vinegar
2 teaspoons sesame oil

Preparation time: 15 minutes
Cooking time: 10 minutes

1. Heat the oil in a wok until smoking. Add the dried chillis and Szechuan pickles, pork and ginger. Stir-fry over the heat for about 1½ minutes, then add the mangetout, Chinese cabbage, red pepper, carrots, beanshoots and garlic. Sprinkle on the salt and stir together for about 2 minutes.
2. Add the chicken stock and continue to stir for another 2 minutes.
3. Mix together the soy sauce, hoisin sauce, red oil, vinegar and sesame oil in a bowl. Pour over the vegetables and pork in the wok and toss all together. Transfer to a serving plate.

From the left: Carp with Hot Bean Paste, Hot-Tossed Shredded Chicken in Red Oil, Yu-Hsiang Pork Ribbons Quick-Fried with Shredded Vegetables

It is characteristic of a Chinese meal to serve both meat and fish, as here. Dishes are always chosen to complement or contrast with each other. The bean curd dish, soft-textured and bland, combines well with these highly spiced dishes. Bean curd, made from soy-bean milk, is a major source of protein for the whole of China and figures largely in all vegetarian dishes. Fresh bean curd can be obtained in Chinese food stores and supermarkets, and is sometimes stocked by delicatessens. Menu serves 4-6.

Braised Bean Curd with Mushrooms

5 tablespoons vegetable oil
225 g (8 oz) mushrooms, sliced
2 cakes bean curd, cut into 2.5 cm (1 inch) cubes
250 ml (8 fl oz) chicken stock
2 tablespoons dark soy sauce
1 teaspoon salt
½ teaspoon sugar
1 tablespoon cornflour
1 tablespoon water
1 teaspoon sesame oil
1 tablespoon red chilli oil
pinch of freshly ground white pepper
1 spring onion, finely chopped

Preparation time: 10 minutes
Cooking time: 8 minutes

1. Heat 4 tablespoons of the oil in a wok and add the mushrooms. Stir-fry for 1 minute, then remove and drain on paper towels.
2. Add the remaining oil and reheat the wok. Fry the bean curd for 1 minute, then return the mushrooms together with the stock, soy sauce, salt and sugar. Bring to the boil and simmer for about 3 minutes. Blend the cornflour and water and stir into the mixture to thicken the sauce. Arrange on a plate and sprinkle on the sesame oil, red chilli oil and spring onions. Serve hot.

From the top: Braised Bean Curd with Mushrooms, Shredded Beef with Celery, Sweet and Sour Fish

Shredded Beef with Celery

50 g (2 oz) cornflour
1½ teaspoons salt
2 egg whites
225 g (8 oz) topside of beef, shredded
600 ml (1 pint) vegetable oil
2 spring onions, finely chopped
2 chillis, finely chopped
2 slices root ginger, peeled and finely chopped
1 head of young celery, cut into 2.5 cm (1 inch) lengths
2 teaspoons yellow bean paste
3 teaspoons hot Szechuan bean paste
2 tablespoons chicken stock
2 teaspoons crushed Szechuan peppercorns
1 teaspoon sesame oil

Preparation time: 15 minutes
Cooking time: 5 minutes

1. Mix together the cornflour, reserving 1 tablespoon, the salt and egg whites. Toss the beef in this mixture.
2. Heat the oil in a wok to 180°C/350°F, or until a cube of bread browns in 30 seconds, and deep-fry the beef for about 2 minutes or until crispy. Remove and drain on paper towels.
3. Pour off the oil leaving about 1 tablespoon to coat the bottom of the wok, and reheat. Add the spring onions, chillis, ginger and celery. Stir-fry for about 1 minute and then add the yellow bean paste, hot bean paste, chicken stock and Szechuan peppercorns. Stir all together and return the beef to the wok.
4. Blend the remaining tablespoon of cornflour with 2 tablespoons of water and stir into the wok to thicken the sauce. Simmer for a further minute and pour onto a plate. Sprinkle on the sesame oil and serve.

Sweet and Sour Fish

8 white fish fillets
1 teaspoon salt
1 tablespoon cornflour
2 eggs, beaten
6 tablespoons vegetable oil
2 spring onions, finely chopped
2 garlic cloves, crushed
2 slices root ginger, finely shredded
4 tablespoons chicken stock
pinch of MSG
1 tablespoon Chinese wine or dry sherry
Sauce:
2 tablespoons sugar
3 tablespoons wine vinegar
2 tablespoons chicken stock
2 tablespoons chilli sauce
1 tablespoon cornflour
2 tablespoons water
3 tablespoons orange juice

1 tablespoon Chinese wine or dry sherry
1 tablespoon soy sauce

Preparation time: 10 minutes
Cooking time: 8 minutes

1. Dust the fish fillets with salt and cornflour, then dip in the beaten egg.
2. Heat the oil in a wok and fry the fish for 2 minutes. Turn the fish over and add the spring onions, garlic, ginger, chicken stock, MSG and wine to the wok. Cover tightly and cook for another minute, then remove the fish and keep warm.
3. Add all the ingredients for the sauce to the wok and bring to the boil, stirring. Lower the heat and return the fish to the wok. Simmer for 2 minutes, then serve.

The crunchy, nutty, spicy taste of the chicken dish is typical of Szechuan. The French beans are very hot — seed the chillis for a milder flavour. Menu serves 4-6.

French Beans with Chilli

干煸四季豆

450 g (1 lb) French beans, topped, tailed and cut in half
1½ tablespoons vegetable oil
2 garlic cloves, crushed
6 chillis, finely chopped
1 tablespoon soy sauce
½ teaspoon sugar
pinch of MSG
½ teaspoon sesame oil

Preparation time: 15 minutes
Cooking time: 5 minutes

1. Blanch the beans, then drain and refresh under cold running water.
2. Set a wok over high heat for 30 seconds, pour in the oil and wait until it is hot. Turn down the heat to moderate, then put in the garlic and red chillis and stir-fry until fragrant.
3. Put in the French beans and stir well. Add the soy sauce, sugar and MSG. Stir-fry for about 3 minutes, until the beans are well seasoned. Sprinkle with sesame oil and serve.

Double-Cooked Pork in Hot Szechuan Sauce

回锅肉

450 g (1 lb) neck of pork
600 ml (1 pint) vegetable oil
2 tablespoons yellow bean paste
2 tablespoons sugar
2 teaspoons soy sauce
2 garlic cloves, crushed
2 chillis, fresh or dried, finely chopped
1 green pepper, cored, seeded and finely sliced
2 spring onions, sliced into 2.5 cm (1 inch) sections
100 g (4 oz) cabbage, finely sliced
1 teaspoon sesame oil

Preparation time: 10 minutes
Cooking time: 28 minutes

1. Cover the pork with water and bring to the boil. Simmer for about 20 minutes or until tender. Drain and cool. Cut into 1 cm (½ inch) cubes.
2. Heat the wok with the oil to 180°C/350°F or until a cube of bread browns in 30 seconds. Add the pork cubes. Cook for 2 minutes, stirring all the time, then remove the pork and drain on paper towels. Pour off the oil.
3. Reheat the wok and add the yellow bean paste, sugar, soy sauce and garlic. Stir-fry together for 2 seconds then put in the chillis, green pepper, spring onions and cabbage. Return the pork to the wok.
4. Stir for another 4 minutes, then sprinkle on the sesame oil and serve.

Hot-Fried Chilli Chicken with Cashew Nuts

宮
保
雞
丁

2 chicken breasts, cut into 1 cm
  (½ inch) cubes
2 tablespoons Chinese wine or dry
  sherry
2 tablespoons soy sauce
1 egg white
2 tablespoons cornflour
pinch of freshly ground white pepper
5 tablespoons vegetable oil
1 garlic clove, crushed
2 chillis, finely chopped
1 red pepper, cored, seeded and cut
  into 1 cm (½ inch) dice
1 green pepper, cored, seeded and cut
  into 1 cm (½ inch) dice
4 water chestnuts, diced
½ tablespoon wine vinegar
1 teaspoon sugar
1 tablespoon hot Szechuan bean
  paste

1 teaspoon sesame oil
pinch of MSG
4 tablespoons water
100 g (4 oz) roasted unsalted
  cashew nuts

**Preparation time: 12 minutes,
  plus marinating
Cooking time: 7 minutes**

1. Mix the chicken cubes in a bowl
with 1 tablespoon wine, 1 tablespoon
soy sauce, 1 egg white, 1 tablespoon
cornflour and a pinch of white pepper.
Leave to marinate for 10 minutes.
2. Heat 4 tablespoons of oil in a wok
until smoking. Drop in the garlic,
chillis and chicken. Stir-fry quickly for
2-3 minutes then remove.

3. Reheat the wok and add the red
and green peppers and water chestnuts. Stir-fry for about 1 minute, then
add to the chicken on the plate.
4. Add the remaining oil and reheat
the wok. Add the remaining soy sauce,
wine, vinegar, sugar, bean sauce,
sesame oil, MSG and the cornflour
blended with the water. Bring to the
boil, stirring, then return the chicken,
peppers and water chestnuts to the
wok. Toss to coat the chicken with the
sauce, then add the cashew nuts.

*From the left: French Beans with Chilli,
Double-Cooked Pork in Hot Szechuan
Sauce, Hot-Fried Chilli Chicken with Cashew
Nuts*
Illustration: A travelling jack-of-all-
trades.

Szechuan is definitely for those who like hot, spicy food. Chillis are used in almost every dish, as here — be sure to seed them if your guests dislike very hot food. Serves 4.

Quick-Fry Hot and Sour Pork

450 g (1 lb) neck of pork, cut into
   matchstick shreds
75 g (3 oz) cornflour
2 eggs
2 tablespoons water
600 ml (1 pint) vegetable oil
2 chillis, finely chopped
2 spring onions, finely chopped
1 red pepper, cored, seeded and diced
5 cm (2 inch) canned bamboo
   shoots, thinly sliced
2 tablespoons chicken stock
1 tablespoon wine vinegar
2 teaspoons tomato ketchup
1 teaspoon salt

Preparation time: 10 minutes
Cooking time: 8 minutes

1. Toss the pork cubes in half the cornflour.
2. Reserve 1 tablespoon of cornflour and mix the remainder with the eggs and water to make a batter. Turn the pork in the batter until well coated.
3. Heat the oil in a wok until smoking, and deep-fry the pork until golden brown. Remove and drain.
4. Pour off all but 1 tablespoon of the oil and reheat. Put in the chillis, spring onions, red pepper and bamboo shoot. Stir-fry all together and then add half the chicken stock, the vinegar, tomato ketchup and salt. Bring to the boil. Blend the remaining cornflour with the remaining stock and stir into the wok, then return the pork to the wok to reheat.

Shredded Chicken and Celery

450 g (1 lb) chicken breast, boned
   and cut into matchstick shreds
1 teaspoon salt
2 egg whites
2 tablespoons cornflour
4 tablespoons vegetable oil
5 slices root ginger, peeled and
   shredded
2 spring onions, shredded
2 sticks celery, shredded
1 chilli, shredded
3 tablespoons soy sauce
2 tablespoons dry sherry

Preparation time: 15 minutes
Cooking time: 5 minutes

Fish Fillets with Chilli and Tomato Sauce

1. Sprinkle the chicken with salt, then toss in the egg white, followed by the cornflour.

2. Heat the oil in a wok and stir-fry the chicken over moderate heat until lightly coloured. Remove the chicken with a slotted spoon and drain on paper towels.

3. Increase the heat. When the oil is very hot and smoking, put in the ginger and spring onions followed by the celery and chilli.

4. Stir continuously for about 30 seconds, then add the chicken with the soy sauce and sherry. Blend well and cook for a further 1 to 1½ minutes, stirring all the time.

1 tablespoon dry sherry
1 egg white
1 tablespoon cornflour
450 g (1 lb) fish fillets (plaice or sole), cut into strips
300 ml (½ pint) vegetable oil
1 garlic clove, finely chopped
1 spring onion, finely chopped
1 slice root ginger, peeled and shredded
½ red pepper or chilli, shredded
Sauce:
200 ml (7 fl oz) chicken stock
1 teaspoon salt
1 teaspoon sugar
2 teaspoons cornflour
2 tablespoons chilli sauce
1 tablespoon tomato purée

Preparation time: 15 minutes, plus marinating
Cooking time: 8 minutes

1. Mix together the sherry, egg white and cornflour, toss the fish strips in the mixture and leave to marinate for about 20 minutes.

2. In a wok heat the oil until hot, then fry the fish strips for 2-3 minutes or until golden, separating them with a pair of chopsticks or a fork. Remove and drain the fish on paper towels.

3. Pour off the oil from the wok. Reheat, then add the garlic, spring onion, ginger and red pepper.

4. Blend together the sauce ingredients, then add to the wok with the fish slices. Stir well over the heat before serving.

From the left: Quick-Fry Hot and Sour Pork, Shredded Chicken and Celery, Fish Fillets with Chilli and Tomato Sauce

Salted cabbage is used extensively in Szechuan cooking. To make salted cabbage, wash and dry the cabbage, cut into quarters, and sprinkle with 4 seeded and chopped dried chillis and 1 tablespoon salt. Pack the cabbage in an earthenware jar or bowl, put a plate or lid on top, and a heavy weight. Leave in a cool place to season for 5 days. The salted cabbage can also be shredded and tossed in a salad or used to flavour soups.

Winter Bamboo Shoots with Salted Cabbage

2½ tablespoons lard
700 g (1½ lb) canned bamboo shoots, drained and sliced
75 g (3 oz) salted cabbage
3 tablespoons chicken stock
2 tablespoons soy sauce
2 tablespoons Chinese wine or dry sherry
1½ tablespoons chicken fat
2 teaspoons cornflour
2 tablespoons water

Preparation time: 20 minutes
Cooking time: 7-8 minutes

1. Heat the lard in a wok, add the bamboo shoots and stir-fry over medium heat for 3 minutes. Add the cabbage, stock, soy sauce and wine and cook over low heat for 3 minutes.
2. Turn the heat to high, add the chicken fat and stir in the cornflour blended with the water. Stir to thicken and serve.

Diced Chicken with Chillis and Peppers

225 g (8 oz) chicken breasts, cut into 2.5 cm (1 inch) cubes
1 teaspoon salt
½ teaspoon freshly ground white pepper
1 tablespoon Chinese wine or dry sherry
75 g (3 oz) cornflour, plus 1 tablespoon
2 egg whites
600 ml (1 pint) vegetable oil
100 g (4 oz) canned bamboo shoots, drained and cubed
2 chillis, finely chopped
2 spring onions, finely chopped
2 slices root ginger, finely chopped
1 garlic clove, crushed
1 teaspoon red bean curd cheese
1 tablespoon chicken stock
1 red pepper, cored, seeded and cut into 2.5 cm (1 inch) cubes
2 teaspoons soy sauce
1 teaspoon sugar

Preparation time: 15 minutes
Cooking time: 8 minutes

1. Mix the chicken cubes in a bowl with ½ teaspoon salt, white pepper, half the wine, 75 g (3 oz) of the cornflour and egg whites.
2. Heat the oil in a wok and add the chicken and bamboo shoot. Stir-fry quickly for about 3 minutes, then remove from the oil and drain on paper towels.
3. Pour off most of the oil, leaving about 1 tablespoon to coat the bottom of the wok. Reheat and add the chillis, spring onions, ginger, garlic, red bean curd, remaining salt, chicken stock, chicken, bamboo shoots, red pepper, soy sauce, sugar and remaining wine. Bring to the boil. Blend the remaining cornflour with 1 tablespoon of water and stir into the wok to thicken the sauce. Serve immediately.

From the top: Winter Bamboo Shoots with Salted Cabbage, Liver in Yu-Hsiang Sauce, Diced Chicken with Chillis and Peppers
Illustration: Splitting bamboo for paper-making.

Liver in Yu-Hsiang Sauce

6 tablespoons vegetable oil
450 g (1 lb) pork or lamb's liver, cut into strips
1½ teaspoons salt
2 tablespoons cornflour
1 egg white
Sauce:
3 slices root ginger, peeled and chopped
3 garlic cloves, crushed
3 spring onions, finely chopped
3 dried chillis, finely chopped
2 tablespoons light soy sauce
2 tablespoons chicken stock
2 tablespoons wine vinegar
2 tablespoons cornflour
3 tablespoons water

Preparation time:
Cooking time:

1. Rub the liver with the salt and a half tablespoon of oil. Dredge with the cornflour then dip into the egg white to coat evenly.
2. Heat the remaining oil in a wok. Add the liver and spread the strips evenly over the surface of the wok. After 1 minute turn to cook on the other side. After another minute remove and drain on paper towels.
3. Add the ginger, garlic, spring onions and chillis to the wok and stir-fry over medium heat for 1 minute. Add the soy sauce, stock and vinegar. Blend the cornflour with the water and stir into the wok to thicken the sauce. Turn up the heat and return the liver to the wok. Stir-fry quickly over high heat for 1 minute, then serve.

Beef appears more often on the menu in Szechuan than in the south or east. This is probably because cattle are used extensively for haulage in the region. The meat is rather tough, but a long slow cooking, as here, renders it tender and full of flavour. During the long steaming the meat juices, suet and highly spiced ground rice blend into a thick gravy. Serves 8.

Lotus Wrapped Long Steamed Beef

2 slices root ginger, peeled and
    shredded
3 tablespoons soy sauce
1 tablespoon hoisin sauce
3 teaspoons salt
½ tablespoon red bean curd cheese
2 teaspoons chilli sauce
1 teaspoon Szechuan peppercorns
½ tablespoon sugar
7 tablespoons ground rice
1.5 kg (3 lb) topside of beef, cut into
    16 large slices
225 g (8 oz) suet, cut into half the
    number of beef slices
1-2 dried lotus leaves, soaked for 30
    minutes

Preparation time: 30 minutes
Cooking time: 3½-4 hours

1. Mix together the ginger, soy sauce, hoisin sauce, salt, bean curd, chilli sauce, pepper, sugar and rice until well blended. Rub this mixture into both sides of the beef slices.
2. Cut the lotus leaves into 8 pieces. Sandwich a piece of suet between 2 slices of beef and wrap in a piece of lotus leaf. Tie with string, if necessary, to secure the parcels.
3. Place the lotus parcels in a heatproof dish, place in a steamer, cover and steam vigorously for 3½-4 hours. Serve from the dish. Each diner opens his parcel at the table and eats with chopsticks out of the parcel.

Clockwise from bottom: Szechuan Chilli Chicken, Lotus Wrapped Long Steamed Beef, Braised Cabbage

Braised Cabbage

1 Chinese cabbage, cut into 7.5 cm
    (3 inch) chunks
3 teaspoons salt
600 ml (1 pint) beef stock
1½ chicken stock cubes

Preparation time: 15 minutes,
    plus seasoning
Cooking time: 5 minutes

1. Place cabbage in a large bowl, sprinkle with the salt and leave to season for 15 minutes.
2. Pour enough boiling water on the cabbage leaves to cover. Leave to poach for 5 minutes, then drain thoroughly.
3. Place the cabbage in a large serving bowl. Bring the stock to the boil, add the crumbled stock cubes and stir thoroughly to dissolve. Pour the stock over the cabbage and serve.

Szechuan Chilli Chicken

1½ teaspoons salt
1 egg white
1½ tablespoons cornflour
5 tablespoons vegetable oil
1 chicken, about 1.5 kg (3 lb), cut
    through the bone into 24 bite-
    sized pieces
2 slices root ginger, peeled and finely
    chopped
2 chillis, finely chopped
2 dried chillis, finely chopped
1½ tablespoons soy sauce
1½ tablespoons wine vinegar

Preparation time: 6 minutes
Cooking time: 8 minutes

1. Mix together the salt, egg white, cornflour and 1 tablespoon of oil. Toss the chicken pieces in this.
2. Heat the remaining oil in a wok until smoking and add the ginger and chillis. Stir-fry for about 30 seconds, then add the chicken. Stir-fry for another 5-6 minutes.
3. Mix together the soy sauce and vinegar and pour into the wok. Stir-fry for another minute then serve.

Illustration: 'The thatched cottage of the inkwell'.

INDEX